CALIFORNIA SKETCHES

BY

O. P. FITZGERALD

" And one upon the West
Turned an eye that would not rest.
For far-off hills whereon his joys had been."

FOURTH EDITION.

NASHVILLE, TENN.:
1880

Notice

In many older books, foxing (or discoloration) occurs and, in some instances, print lightens with wear and age. Reprinted books, such as this, often duplicate these flaws, notwithstanding efforts to reduce or eliminate them. The pages of this reprint have been digitally enhanced and, where possible, the flaws eliminated in order to provide clarity of content and a pleasant reading experience.

Copyright © 1879 by O. P. Fitzgerald

Originally published:
Nashville, Tennessee
1880

Reprinted:
Janaway Publishing, Inc.
2011

Janaway Publishing, Inc.
732 Kelsey Ct.
Santa Maria, California 93454
(805) 925-1038
www.janawaygenealogy.com

ISBN: 978-1-59641-239-2

Made in the United States of America

Author's Preface.

THESE Sketches wrote themselves, as it were. About three years ago my friend, Prof. Alonzo Phelps (formerly of Harvard University), in reply to my remark that somebody ought to preserve the vanishing phases of the early California life, said, "Yes, it ought to be done, and you are the man to do it." The matter was then dismissed from my mind as the flattering suggestion of a partial friend. After leaving California, every thing connected with my life, or that had come under my observation while there, assumed a fresh interest to my own mind. The remark of my friend was remembered, and, more to gratify a kindly impulse than with a view to make a volume, in snatches of such leisure as an editor gets, the penciling of these humble Sketches began. Now that the little book is finished, I am at least half sorry it was ever begun. Yet there has been a pleasure in writing it. The old days have come back to me again, and images that were fading have stood before me in the form and color of life. Ah! if I could make them stand thus before my kind readers! The Sketches are all from real life. In one or two instances names are disguised for obvious reasons. I have told the story as I saw it, and as I remember it. There is no fancy-sketch among these chapters. If I had entered that field, a volume more suited to the modern taste might have been the result; but it would have had no value as a picture of actual life. An anachronism may be found here or there. I wrote wholly from memory, and am not strong in the matter of dates. Except incidentally, no mention is made of persons still living, though the promptings of affectionate admiration made a strong temptation to place some living faces on the canvas.

My motive in publishing in this form is not a bad one. It is not literary ambition; for I am conscious that the risk is equal to the possible gain in that direction. It is not to put a shadow upon the memory of the dead, or to inflict a pang upon a living soul. My motive is such as all noble spirits would approve, but which need not be stated here. With these words I send forth my little book, leaving it to its fate.

One of these chapters is from a different hand. Which one it is, is left to the discrimination of the critical reader.

O. P. FITZGERALD.

Nashville, September, 1879.

Contents.

	PAGE
My First Sunday in the Mines	7
Cissaha	14
A Youthful Desperado	28
A Woman of the Early Days	33
Lost on Table Mountain	41
Fulton	52
Blighted	59
Stranded	65
Lockley	72
Father Cox	81
An Interview	89
Stewart	97
The Ethics of Grizzly Hunting	107
A Mendocino Murder	114
Ben	120
Old Tuolumne	124
The Blue Lakes	127
A California Mountain Road	133
Dr. Eleazar Thomas	135
Father Acolti	144
My First California Camp-Meeting	150
The Tragedy at Algerine	160
California Traits	168
California Weddings	182
North Beach, San Francisco	197
St. Helen's at Sunrise	208

MY FIRST SUNDAY IN THE MINES.

SONORA, in 1855, was an exciting, wild, wicked, fascinating place. Gold-dust and gamblers were plentiful. A rich mining camp is a bonanza to the sporting fraternity. The peculiar excitement of mining is near akin to gambling, and seems to prepare the gold-hunter for the faro-bank and monte-table. The life was free and spiced with tragedy. The men were reckless, the women few and not wholly select. The conventionalities of older communities were ignored. People dressed and talked as they pleased, and were a law unto themselves. Even a parson could gallop at full speed through a mining camp without exciting remark. To me it was all new, and at first a little bewildering, but there was a charm about it that lingers pleasantly in the memory after the lapse of all these long years from 1855 to 1879.

Sonora was a picture unique in its beauty as I

first looked down upon it from the crest of the highest hill above the town that bright May morning. The air exhilarated like wine. The sky was deep blue without a speck of cloud. The town lay stretched between two ranges of hills, the cozy cottages and rude cabins straggling along their sides, while the full tide of life flowed through Washington street in the center, where thousands of miners jostled one another as they moved to and fro. High hills encircled the place on all sides protectingly, and Bald Mountain, dark and bare, lifted above all the rest, seemed to watch the queen city of the mines like a dusky duenna. The far-off Sierras, white and cold, lay propped against the sky like shrouded giants under their winding-sheets of snow. Near me stood a lone pine which had escaped the ruthless ax because there was a grave under it marked by a rude cross.

Descending to the main street again, I found it crowded with flannel-shirted men. They seemed to be excited, judging from their loud tones and fierce gesticulations.

"They have caught Felipe at French Camp, and they will have him here by ten o'clock," said one of a group near me.

"Yes, and the boys are getting ready to swing the —— greaser when he gets here," said another, savagely.

My First Sunday in the Mines.

On inquiry, I learned that the gentleman for whose arrival such preparation was being made was a Mexican who had stabbed to the heart a policeman named Sheldon two nights before. The assassin fled the town, but the sheriff and his posse had gotten on his track, and, pursuing rapidly, had overtaken him at French Camp, and were now returning with their prisoner in charge. Sheldon was a good-natured, generous fellow, popular with the "boys." He was brave to a fault, perhaps a little too ready at times to use his pistol. Two Mexicans had been shot by him since his call to police duty, and though the Americans justified him in so doing, the Mexicans cherished a bitter feeling toward him. Sheldon knew that he was hated by those swarthy fellows whose strong point is not forgiveness of enemies, and not long before the tragedy was heard to say, in a half-serious tone, "I expect to die in my boots." Poor fellow! it came sooner than he thought.

By ten o'clock Washington street was densely thronged by red and blue-shirted men, whose remarks showed that they were ripe for mischief.

"Hang him, I say! If we allow the officers who watch for our protection when we are asleep to be murdered in this way nobody is safe. I say hang him!" shouted a thick-chested miner, gritting his teeth.

"That's the talk! swing him!" "Hang him!" "Put cold lead through him!" and such like expressions were heard on all sides.

Suddenly there was a rush of the crowd toward the point where Washington street intersected with the Jamestown road. Then the tide flowed backward, and came surging by the place where I was standing.

"There he comes! at him, boys!" "A rope! a rope!" "Go for him!" shouted a hundred voices.

The object of the popular execration, guarded by the sheriff and posse of about twenty men, was hurried along in the middle of the street, his hat gone, his bosom bare, a red sash round his waist. He was a bad-looking fellow, and in the rapid glances he cast at the angry crowd around him there was more of hate than fear. The flashes of his dark eyes made one think of the gleam of the deadly Spanish dirk. The twenty picked men guarding him had each a revolver in his hand, with Major Solomon, the sheriff, at their head. The mob knew Solomon. He had distinguished himself for cool courage in the Mexican war, and they were well aware that those pistols were paraded for use if occasion demanded.

The prisoner was taken into the Placer Hotel, where the coroner's jury was held, the mob surrounding the building and roaring like a sea.

"There they come! go for him, boys!" was shouted as the doors were flung open, and Felipe appeared, attended by his guard.

A rush was made, but there was Solomon with his twenty men pistol in hand, and no man dared to lay a hand on the murderer. With steady step they marched to the jail, the crowd parting as the sheriff and his posse advanced, and the prisoner was hurried inside and the doors locked.

Baffled thus, for a few moments the mob was silent, and then it exploded with imprecations and yells.

"Break open the door!" "Tear down the jail!" "Bring him out!" "Who has a rope?" "Out with him!"

Cool and collected, Solomon stood on the doorstep, his twenty men standing holding their revolvers ready. The County Judge Quint attempted to address the excited mass, but his voice was drowned by their yells. The silver-tongued Henry P. Barber, an orator born, and whose sad career would make a romance of thrilling interest, essayed to speak, but even his magic voice was lost in the tornado of popular fury.

I had climbed a high fence above the jail-yard, where the whole scene was before me. When Barber gave up the attempt to get a hearing from the mob, there was a momentary silence. Solomon saw the opportunity, and lifting his hand, he said:

"Will you hear me a moment? I am not fool enough to think that with these twenty men I can whip this crowd. You can overcome us by your numbers and kill us if you choose. Perhaps you will do it—I am ready for that. I don't say I can prevent you, but I do say [and here his eye kindled and his voice had a steel-like ring] *the first man that touches that jail-door dies!*"

There was a perceptible thrill throughout that dense mass of human beings. No man volunteered to lead an assault on the jail-door. Solomon followed up this stroke:

"Boys, when you take time to reflect, you will see that this is all wrong. I was elected by your votes, and you are acting in bad faith when you put me in a position where I must violate my sworn duty or fight you. This is the holy Sabbath-day. Back in our old homes we have been used to different scenes from this. The prisoner will be kept, and tried, and duly punished by the law. Let us give three cheers for the clergy of California, two of whom I see present [pointing to where my Presbyterian neighbor, the Rev. S. S. Harmon, and I were perched conspicuously], and then go home like good citizens."

Courage and tact prevailed. The mob was con-

My First Sunday in the Mines.

quered. The cheers were given with a will, the crowd melted away, and in a few minutes the jail-yard was clear.

I lingered alone, and was struck with the sudden transition. The sun was sinking in the west, already the town below was wrapped in shade, the tops of the encircling hills caught the lingering beams, the loftier crest of Bald Mountain blazing as if it were a mass of burnished gold. It was the calm and glory of nature in sharp contrast with the turbulence and brutality of men.

Wending my way back to the hotel, I seated myself on the piazza of the second story, and watched the motley crowd going in and out of the "Long Tom" drinking and gambling saloon across the street, musing upon the scenes of my first Sunday in the mines.

CISSAHA.

FIRST noticed him one night at a prayer-meeting at Sonora, in the Southern Mines, in 1855. He came in timidly, and took a seat near the door. His manner was reverent, and he watched the exercises with curious interest, his eyes following every gesture of the preacher, and his ears losing not a word that was said or sung. I was struck with his peculiar physiognomy as he sat there with his thin, swarthy face, his soft, sad, black eyes, and long black hair. I could not make him out; he might be Mexican, Spanish, Portuguese, "Kanaka," or what not. He waited until I passed out at the close of the meeting, and, bowing very humbly, placed half a dollar in my hand, and walked away. This happened several weeks in succession, and I noticed him at church on Sunday evenings. He would come in after the crowd had entered, and take his place near the door. He never failed to hand me the half dollar at the close of every service, his dark, wistful-looking eyes lighting up with pleasure as I took the coin from his hand. He never waited to talk, but hurried off at once. My curiosity was excited, and I began to feel a special interest in this strange-looking foreigner.

I was sitting one morning in the little room on the hill-side, which was at once dining-room, parlor, bed-chamber, and study, when, lifting my eyes a moment from the book I was reading, there stood my strange foreigner in the door.

"Come in," I said kindly.

Making profound salaams, he rushed impulsively toward me, exclaiming in broken English—

"My good brahmin! My good brahmin!" with a torrent of words that I could not understand.

I invited him to take a seat, but he declined. He looked flushed and excited, his dark eyes flashing. I soon found that he could understand English much better than he could speak it himself.

"What is your name?" I asked.

"Cissaha," he answered, accenting strongly the last syllable.

"Of what nation are you?" was my next question.

"Me Hindoo—me good caste," he added rather proudly.

After gratifying my curiosity by answering my

many questions, he told his business with me. It was with great difficulty that I could make out what he said; his pronunciation was sadly imperfect at best, and when he talked himself into an excited state, his speech was a terrible jargon of confused and strange sounds. The substance of his story was, that, though belonging to a caste which was above such work, necessity had forced him to take the place of a cook in a miner's boarding-house at a notorious camp called aptly Whisky Hill, which was about three miles from Sonora. After six months' service, the proprietor of the establishment had dismissed him with no other pay than a bogus title to a mining claim. When the poor fellow went to take possession, the rightful owners drove him away with many blows and much of that peculiarly emphatic profanity for which California was rather noted in those early days. On going back to his employer with the story of his failure to get possession of the mining claim, he was driven away with cursing and threats, without a dollar for months of hard work.

This was Cissaha's story. He had come to me for redress. I felt no little sympathy for him as he stood before me, so helpless in a strange land. He had been shamefully wronged, and I felt indignant at the recital. But I told him that while I was sorry for him, I could do nothing; he had better put the case in the hands of a lawyer. I suggested the name of one.

"No, no!" he said passionately; "you my good brahmin; you go Whisky Hill, you make Flank Powell pay my money!"

He seemed to think that as a teacher of religion I must be invested also with some sort of authority in civil matters. I could not make him understand that this was not so.

"You ride horse, me walk; Flank Powell see my good brahmin come, he pay money," urged Cissaha.

Yielding to a sudden impulse, I told him I would go with him. He bowed almost to the floor, and the tears, which had flowed freely as he told his tale of wrongs, were wiped away.

Mounting Dr. Jack Franklin's sorrel horse—my pen pauses as I write the name of that noble Tennessean, that true and generous friend—I started to Whisky Hill, my client keeping alongside on foot.

As we proceeded, I could not help feeling that I was on a sort of fool's errand. It was certainly a new *role* for me. But my sympathy had been excited, and I fortified myself by repeating mentally all those scriptures of the Old and New Testaments which enjoin kindness to strangers.

I found that Cissaha was well known in the

camp, and that he was generally liked. Everybody seemed to know how he had been treated, and the popular feeling was on his side. Several parties confirmed his statement of the case in every particular. Walking along among the mining claims, with a proud and confident air, he would point to me, saying—

"There my good brahmin—*he* make Flank Powell pay my money now."

"Powell is a rough customer," said a tall young fellow from New York, who stood near the trail with a pick in his hand; "he will give you trouble before you get through with him."

Cissaha only shook his head in a knowing way and hastened on, keeping my sorrel in a brisk little trot.

A stout and ill-dressed woman was standing in the porch of Mr. Powell's establishment as I rode up.

"Is Mr. Powell at home?" I asked.

"Yes, he is in the house," she said dryly, scowling alternately at Cissaha and me.

"Please tell him that I would like to see him."

She went into the house after giving us a parting angry glance, and in a few minutes Mr. Powell made his appearance. He looked the ruffian that he was all over. A huge fellow, with enormous breadth between the shoulders, and the chest of a bull, with a fiery red face, blear blue eyes red at the corners, coarse sandy hair, and a villainous *tout ensemble* every way, he was as bad a specimen of my kind as I had ever met.

"What do you want with me?" he growled out after taking a look at us.

"I understand," I answered in my blandest tones, "that there has been some difficulty in making a settlement between you and this Hindoo man, and at his request I have come over to see if I can help to adjust it."

"—— you!" said the ruffian, "if you come here meddling with my affairs I'll knock you off that horse."

He *was* a rough customer to look at just then.

Cissaha looked a little alarmed, and drew nearer to me.

I looked the man in the eye and answered—

"I am not afraid of any violence at your hands. You dare not attempt it. You have cruelly wronged this poor foreigner, and you know it. Every man in the camp condemns you for it, and is ashamed of your conduct. Now, I intend to see this thing through. I will devote a year to it and spend every dollar I can raise if necessary to make you pay this debt!"

By this time quite a crowd of miners had gathered around us, and there were unmistakable expressions of approval of my speech.

"That's the right sort of talk!" exclaimed a grizzly-bearded man in a red shirt.

"Stand up to him, parson!" said another.

There was a pause. Powell, as I learned afterward, was detested in the camp. He had the reputation of a bully and a cheat. I think he was likewise a coward. At any rate, as I warmed with virtuous indignation, he cooled. Perhaps he did not like the expressions on the faces of the rough, athletic men standing around.

"What do you want me to do?" he asked in a sullen tone.

"I want you to pay this man what you owe him," I answered.

The negotiations begun thus unpromisingly ended very happily. After making some deduction on some pretext or other, the money was paid, much to my relief and the joy of my client. Mr. Powell indulged in no parting courtesies, nor did he tender me the hospitalities of his house. I have never seen him from that day to this. I have never wished to renew his acquaintance.

Cissaha marched back to Sonora in triumph.

A few days after the Whisky Hill adventure, as I was sitting on the rear side of the little parsonage to get the benefit of the shade, I had another visit from Cissaha. He had on his shoulder a miner's pick and shovel, which he laid down at my feet.

"What is that for?" I asked.

"My good brahmin look at pick and shobel, then no break, and find heap gold," said he, his face full of trust and hopefulness.

I cast a kindly glance at the implements, and did not think it worth while to combat his innocent superstition. If good wishes could have brought him good luck the poor fellow would have prospered in his search after gold.

From that time on he was scarcely ever absent from church services, never omitting to pay his weekly half dollar. More than once I observed the tears running down his cheeks as he sat near the door, eye and ear all attent to the service.

A day or two before my departure for Conference, at the end of my two years in Sonora, Cissaha made me a visit. He looked sad and anxious.

"You go way?" he inquired.

"Yes, I must go," I answered.

"You no come back Sonora?" he asked.

"No; I cannot come back," I said.

He stood a moment, his chest heaving with emotion, and then said—

"Me go with you, me live where you live, me die where you die"—almost the very words of the fair young Moabite.

Cissaha went with us. How could I refuse to take him? At San Jose he lived with us, doing our cooking, nursing our little Paul, and making himself generally useful. He taught us to love curry and to eat cucumbers Hindoo fashion—that is, stewed with veal or chicken. He was the gentlest and most docile of servants, never out of temper, and always anxious to please. Little Paul was very fond of him, and often he would take him off in his baby-wagon, and they would be gone for hours together.

He never tired asking questions about the Christian religion, and manifested a peculiar delight in the words and life of Jesus. One day he came into my study and said—

"Me want you to make me Christian."

"I can't make you a Christian—Jesus can do it," I answered.

He looked greatly puzzled and troubled at this reply, but when I had explained the whole matter to him, he brightened up and intimated that he wanted to join the Church. I enrolled his name as a probationer, and his delight was unbounded.

One day Cissaha came to me all smiling, and said—

"Me want to give all the preachers one big dinner."

"Very well," I answered; "I will let you do so. How many do you want?"

"Me want heap preachers, table all full," he said.

He gave me to understand that the feast must be altogether his own—his money must buy every thing, even to the salt and pepper for seasoning the dishes. He would use nothing that was in the house, but bought flour, fowls, beef, vegetables, confectionery, coffee, tea, every thing for the great occasion. He made a grand dinner, not forgetting the curry, and with a table full of preachers to enjoy it, he was a picture of happiness. His dark face beamed with delight as he handed around the viands to the smiling and appreciative guests. He had some Hindoo notion that there was great merit in feasting so many belonging to the brahmin caste. To him the dinner was a sort of sacrifice most acceptable to Heaven.

My oriental domestic seemed very happy for some months, and became a general favorite on account of his gentle manners, docile temper, and obliging disposition. His name was shortened to "Tom" by the popular usage, and under the instructions of the mistress of the parsonage he began the study of English. Poor fellow! he never could make the sound of f or z, the former always turning to *p*, and the latter to *g*, upon his tongue. I believe there are no p's or g's in the Hindoostanee.

A change came over Cissaha. He became all at once moody and silent. Several times I found him in tears. Something was the matter with him, that was clear.

One afternoon the secret came out. He came into my room. There were traces of tears on his cheeks.

"I go 'way—can stay with my pather [father] no more," he said, with a quiver in his voice.

"Why, what is the matter?" I asked.

"Debbil in here," he answered, touching his forehead. "Debbil tell me drink whisky; me no drink where my pather stay, so must go."

"Why, I did not know you ever drank whisky; where did you learn that?" I asked.

"Me drink with the boys at Flank Powell's—drink beer and whisky. No drink for long time, but debbil in here [touching his forehead] say *must* drink."

He was a picture of shame and grief as he stood there before me. How hard he must have fought against the appetite for strong drink since he had been with me!—and how full of shame and sorrow he was to confess his weakness to me! He told me all about it—how he had been treated to beer and whisky by the good-natured miners, and how the taste for liquor had grown on him, and how he had resisted for a time, and how he had at last yielded to the feeling that the devil was too strong for him. That the devil was in it, he seemed to have no doubt. And truly it was so—the cruelest, deadliest of devils, the devil of drink! As a Hindoo, in his own country no strong drink had ever passed his lips. The fiery potations of Whisky Hill were too much for him.

"You should pray, Cissaha."

"Me pray all night, but debbil too strong—me *must* drink whisky!" he said vehemently.

He left us. The parting was very sad to him and us. He had a special cry over little Paul.

"You my pather [to me]; you my mother [to my wife]; I go, but me pack you both always in my belly!"

We could but smile through our tears. The poor fellow meant to say he would still bear us in his grateful heart in his wanderings.

After a few months he came to see us. He looked seedy and sad. He had found employment, but did not stay long at a place. He had stopped awhile with a Presbyterian minister in the Sacramento Valley, and was solicited by him to join the Church.

"Me tell him no!" he said, his eye flashing; "me tell him my pather done make me Christian; me no want to be made Christian again."

The poor fellow was true to his first love, sad Christian as he was.

"Me drink no whisky for four, five week—me

now try to stop. Give me prayer to say when debbil get in here"—touching his head.

That was what he had come for chiefly. I gave him the form of a short and simple prayer. He repeated it after me in his way until he had it by heart, and then he left.

Once or twice a year he came to see us, and always had a pathetic tale to tell of his struggles with strong drink, and the greed and violence of men who were tempted to oppress and maltreat a poor creature whose weakness invited injustice.

He told us of an adventure when acting as a sheep-herder in Southern California, whither he had wandered. A large flock of sheep which he had in charge had been disturbed in the corral a couple of nights in succession. On the third night, hearing a commotion among them, he sprang up from his bunk and rushed out to see what was the matter. But let him tell the story:

"Me run out to see what's matter; stars shine blight; me get into corral; sheep all bery much scared, and bery much run, and bery much jump. Big black bear jump over corral fence and come right for me. Me so flighten me know nothing, but raise my arms, run at bear, and say, *E-e-c-e-e-e!*" prolonging the shrill scream and becoming terribly excited as he went on.

"Well, how did it end?" I asked.

"Me scream so loud that bear get scared too, and he turn, run bery fast, jump over corral, and run away."

We did not doubt this story. The narration was too vivid to have been invented, and that scream was enough to upset the nerves of any grizzly.

We got to looking for him at regular intervals. He would bring candies and little presents for the children, and would give a tearful recital of his experiences and take a tearful leave of us. He was fighting his enemy and still claiming to be a Christian. He said many things which showed that he had thought earnestly and deeply on religious subjects, and he would end by saying, "Jesus, help me! Jesus, help me!"

He came to see us after the death of our Paul, and he wept when we told him how our dear boy had left us. He had had a long sickness in the hospital. He had before expressed a desire to go back to his own country, and now this desire had grown into a passion. His wan face lighted up as he looked wistfully seaward from the bay-window of our cottage on the hill above the Golden Gate. He left us with a slow and feeble step, often looking back as long as he was in sight.

That was the last of Cissaha. I know not whether he is in Hindostan or the world of spirits.

A YOUTHFUL DESPERADO.

"THERE'S a young chap in the jail over there you ought to go and see. It's the one who killed the two Chinamen on Woods's Creek, a few weeks ago. He goes by the name of Tom Ellis. He is scarcely more than a boy, but he is a hard one. May be you can do him some good."

This was said to me by one of the sheriff's deputies, a kind-hearted fellow, but brave as a lion— one of those quiet, low-voiced men who do the most daring things in a matter-of-course way—a man who never made threats and never showed a weapon except when he was about to use it with deadly effect.

The next day I went over to see the young murderer. I was startled at his youthful appearance, and struck with his beauty. His features were feminine in their delicacy, and his skin was almost as soft and fair as a child's. He had dark hair,

A Youthful Desperado.

bright blue eyes, and white teeth. He was of medium size, and was faultless in *physique*. Though heavily ironed, his step was vigorous and springy, indicating unusual strength and agility.

This fair-faced, almost girlish youth, had committed one of the most atrocious double murders ever known. Approaching two Chinamen who were working an abandoned mining claim on the creek, he demanded their gold-dust, exhibiting at the same time a Bowie-knife. The Chinamen, terrified, dropped their mining tools and fled, pursued by the young devil, who, fleet of foot, soon overtook the poor creatures, and with repeated stabs in the back cut them down. A passer-by found him engaged in rifling their pockets of the gold-dust, to the value of about twenty dollars, which had tempted him to commit the horrid crime.

These were the facts in the case, as brought out in the trial. It was also shown that he had borne a very bad name, associating with the worst characters, and being suspected strongly of other crimes against life and property. He was convicted and sentenced to death.

This was the man I had come to see. He received me politely, but I made little progress in my attempt to turn his thoughts to the subject of preparation for death. He allowed me to read the Bible in his cell and pray for him, but I could see plainly enough that he took no interest in it. I left a Bible with him, with the leaves turned down to mark such portions of the word of God as would be most likely to do him good, and he promised to read it, but it was evident he did not do it. For weeks I tried in every possible way to reach his conscience and sensibilities, but in vain. I asked him one day—

"Have you a mother living?"

"Yes; she lives in Ohio, and is a member of the Baptist Church."

"Does she know where you are?"

"No—she thinks I'm dead, and she will never know any better. It's just as well—it would do the old lady no good. The name I go by here is not my real name—no man in California knows my true name."

Even this chord did not respond. He was as cold and hard as ice. I kept up my visits to him, and continued my efforts to win him to thoughts suitable to his condition, but he never showed the least sign of penitence or feeling of any kind. He was the only human being I have ever met who did not have a tender spot somewhere in his nature. If he had any such spot, my poor skill failed to discover it.

One day, after I had spent an hour or more with him, he said to me—

"You mean well in coming here to see me, and I'm always glad to see you, as I get very lonesome, but there's no use in keeping up any deception about the matter. I don't care any thing about religion, and all your talk on that subject is wasted. But if you could help me to get out of this jail, so that I could kill the man whose evidence convicted me, I would thank you. —— him! I would be willing to die if I could kill him first!"

As he spoke his eye glittered like a serpent's, and I felt that I was in the presence of a fiend. From this time on there was no disguise on his part; he thirsted for blood, and hated to die chiefly because it cut him off from his revenge. He did not deny the commission of the murders, and cared no more for it than he would for the shooting of a rabbit. As a psychological study, this fair young devil profoundly interested me, and I sought to learn more of his history, that I might know how much of his fiendishness was due to organic tendency, and how much to evil association. But he would tell nothing of his former life, and I was left to conjecture as to what were the influences that had so completely blasted every bud and blossom of good in one so young. And he was so handsome!

He made several desperate attempts to break jail, and was loaded down with extra irons and put under special guard. The night before his execution he slept soundly, and ate a hearty breakfast next morning. At the gallows he showed no fear or emotion of any kind. He was brooding on his revenge to the last moment. "It is well for Short that I did n't get out of this—I would like to live long enough to kill him!" were about the last words he uttered, in a sort of soliloquizing way. The black cap was drawn over his fair, handsome face, and without a quiver of the nerves, or the least tremor of the pulse, he was launched into the world of spirits, in the midst of a rabble who looked on with mingled curiosity, awe, and pity.

A WOMAN OF THE EARLY DAYS.

ONE day in the summer of 1856, I was called to attend a wedding in the city of Sonora. At the appointed hour I repaired to the house designated, a neat little cottage surrounded with flowers and shrubbery. A pleasant party had already assembled in the snug little parlor. In a few minutes the bridegroom entered the room. He was a fine specimen of manly beauty. He had a faultless figure, a handsome, winning face, and graceful manners, a little dashed with Californian *abandon*. After a little conversation he left the room, and soon returned, presenting himself with the bride, ready for the ceremony. She was very beautiful; her form was perfectly rounded, a model for an artist, her face fair and sunny, shaded by luxuriant dark, clustering hair, her eyes large and lustrous. They were both radiant with happiness, and it was a merry party that sat down to the elegant dinner which followed the bridal ceremony.

This marriage made a brief sensation. The parties were both well known, and the bride's California life made one of those romantic episodes so common in those early days. The romance, alas! was too often tinged with the darker colors of sin. So it was in this case. This is the story of Kate S——, as told to me by herself:

"I was the youngest child of a happy family near L——, in Pennsylvania. I was called pretty, and was the pet of the household. When I was scarcely sixteen, while still a school-girl, a wealthy neighbor proposed to marry me. My father favored the proposal. I was startled by it, and told my father I did not and could not love him, and would not marry him. My lover persisted in his addresses, my father seconding his suit, and at last I consented to wed him. O how bitterly have I rued the day! I could not love him, and I soon ceased to respect him. He was cold, selfish, and jealous. He petted and flattered me at first, but soon discovering that I did not love him, and only endured his caresses, his conduct changed into systematic injustice and oppression. When a child was born to us, I tried to love him for its sake. I tried to do my duty as a wife, but was unhappy, despite the wealth for which I had been sold. My husband's business took an unfortunate turn, and he lost nearly all he had. Then he became still more unkind to me, while at the same time I was denied many of the comforts and luxuries to which I had become accustomed.

"In 1849 he suddenly avowed his purpose to go to California, and started at once, leaving me with my father. He had been in California about a year, when he wrote to me, giving an encouraging account of his success, asking me to go to him, and promising to do every thing in his power to make me happy. I thought it my duty to go, still indulging a lingering hope that he might be a different man, and that we might yet be happy.

"I wrote to him, telling him when I would start, and asking him to meet me in San Francisco on my arrival. When we passed through the Golden Gate, entered the bay, and landed at the wharf, I looked in vain for him among the crowds in waiting. He was not there—every face was strange. After waiting in San Francisco two days, I proceeded to Sonora, whence his letters had been written, having barely money enough to meet the expense of the journey.

"On my arrival at Sonora, I learned that he was in the vicinity, and sent for him. He came, but greeted me coldly, though he seemed glad to see the child, then six years old. He engaged board for me at a hotel, but left the place without paying. When the bill was presented to me, having no money to pay it, I offered to hire myself to the hotel-keeper as a servant, and my offer was accepted. My husband did not come near me. I learned the reason: he had left, in company with a disreputable woman, not even taking leave of his child. My duties as a servant were not very laborious, but I felt humiliated and heart-broken.

"Sonora was then almost one great gambling-hell. Almost everybody gambled. The dealers of the games were mostly women. The largest gambling-hell in the city belonged to an old man, one of its most influential citizens. I was surprised when he came to me one day and proposed to employ me as a monte-dealer. I shrank from the proposal. He offered me large wages, and promised to protect me as his own daughter. At last I yielded, and was soon regularly dealing cards at a monte-table. My employer was delighted with the result. Crowds were gathered nightly round the table at which I presided. I was utterly miserable. I loathed the very sight of the money I made so rapidly. Many fearful scenes did I witness in that gambling-hell—men shot dead over the table at which I sat, young men stripped of their last dollar, rushing out desperate, ready for robbery or suicide, old men cursing their luck with clenched hands, and tearing their gray hairs in frenzy—it is horrible to think of it!

"It was here that I met Frank B——. He was a gambler of the more gentlemanly sort, and I met him frequently. I was constantly exposed to insults from the drunken and half-drunken men who frequented the place. One night a burly ruffian was more grossly insulting than was usual. Frank B—— was standing near, and quick as thought felled him to the floor with a heavy blow of a loaded cane which he always carried. The desperado rose to his feet furious with rage, and drawing a Bowie-knife rushed upon Frank, but he was seized, disarmed, and thrust out into the street, after rough handling by a dozen strong men.

"Not long after this occurrence, Frank proposed to marry me. I already knew that I loved him, but I told him that I was a married woman, and could not listen to him. Steps were taken to procure a divorce. By his advice I left the gambling-hell, and was full of joy at my release.

"Pending the proceedings for divorce, I went to San Francisco, where I passed through temptations and troubles of a very painful character, but which I would forever forget if I could. At length, the divorce having been effected, I returned to Sonora, where I have lived until now. It seems as if a dark and troubled dream had passed away, and I had awoke to a bright and happy morning."

After their marriage, they seemed to be perfectly

happy. No two individuals ever seemed to be more evidently designed by nature for each other. I learned that Frank B—— had been respectably bred and liberally educated. Since coming to California he had at one time amassed a large fortune, but had lost it by indulging his passion for gambling. From being their victim, he had now become the associate and confederate of the gambling fraternity. But he was disgusted with the life he was leading, and told me that he intended to abandon it.

"Good news!" said she to me one day as I entered the cottage. "Good news! Frank has got a deputyship in one of the county offices, and will change his life."

Tears of joy were in her eyes as she told me, and my congratulations were most hearty. In a few days he entered upon his new employment with a hopeful and happy heart. When I met him in the streets he seemed to walk more erect, and his eye met mine with a more manly and independent expression. Handsome before, now he looked noble.

Only a few weeks had elapsed when, having visited a town some twelve miles distant, he was seized with a fever and was brought home in a state of delirium. His wife had a presentiment from the first that the attack would be fatal. He seemed to have a similar feeling. In his lucid intervals he spoke to her with a mournful tenderness of their approaching separation. In little more than a week he died, and a great concourse of men and a few women gathered on the hill to see him buried.

The blow was a terrible one to her. Her grief was so wild and fearful that even feminine criticism was awed into silence or melted into sympathy. Frank's sudden death, and his wife's anguish, broke down the barriers which had previously limited her social life, and she was made to feel the throb of the sympathetic heart of the place. Conventionalities were swept away by the breath of sorrow. The only women who held aloof from the mourner were those who had a painful consciousness that their own social standing was somewhat equivocal.

I visited her, and sought to point her to the Source of true consolation. She interrupted me by demanding fiercely—her eyes fairly blazing—

"Do you think my husband is in heaven?"

Not giving me time to answer, she continued in a defiant tone, walking the floor as she spoke, her long hair disheveled, and her hands clasped—

"Don't speak to me of religion, unless you can tell me *he* is happy! If *he* is not saved, I do not wish to be! *Where he is—no higher, no lower—is my heaven!*"

She fought a hard battle with poverty and temptation in the mines, drifted down to San Francisco, still looking young and beautiful, and—shall I spoil a romance by telling it?—married a rich man, and is living in luxury. But I choose to believe all the heart she had to give was buried in Frank B——'s grave on the hill above Sonora.

LOST ON TABLE MOUNTAIN.

TABLE Mountain is a geological curiosity. It has puzzled the scientists, excited the wonder of the vulgar, and aroused the cupidity of the gold-hunter. It is a river without water, a river without banks, a river whose bed is hundreds of feet in the air. Rising in Calaveras county, it runs southward more than a hundred miles, winding gracefully in its course, and passing through what was one of the richest gold-belts in the world. But now the bustling camps are still, the thousands who delved the earth for the shining ore are gone, the very houses have disappeared. The scarred bosom of Mother Earth alone tells of the intensely passionate life that once throbbed among these rocky hills. A deserted mining-camp is in more senses than one like a battle-field. Both leave the same tragic impression upon the mind.

What is now Table Mountain was many ages ago a river flowing from the foot of the Sierras into the

San Joaquin Valley. A volcano at its head discharged its lava into it, and it slowly rolled down its bed, and cooling, left the hard volcanic matter to resist the action of the elements by which the surrounding country was worn away, until it was left high in the air, a phenomenon to exercise the wits of the learned, and a delight to the lover of the curious in Nature.

I can modestly claim the honor of having preached the first sermon on the south side of Table Mountain, where Mormon Creek was thronged with miners, who filled Davy Jamison's dining-room to attend religious service on Wednesday nights. It was a big day for us all when we dedicated a board-house to the worship of God and the instruction of youth. It was both church and school-house. I have still a very vivid remembrance of that occasion. My audience was composed of the gold-diggers on the creek, with half a dozen women and nearly as many babies, who insisted on being heard as well as the preacher. I "kept the floor" until two long, lean yellow dogs had a disagreement, showed their teeth, erected their bristles, sidled up closer and closer, growling, until they suddenly flew at each other like tigers, and fought all over the house. My plan was not to notice the dogs, and so elevating my voice, I kept on speaking. The dogs snapped and bit fearfully, the women screamed, the children became frantic, stiffening themselves and turning purple in the face; a bushy-whiskered man with a red head kicked the dogs from him with loud imprecations, while Davy Jamison used a long broom upon them with great energy, but with unsatisfactory result. Those yellow dogs were mad, and didn't care for kicks or brooms. They stuck to each other, and fought over and under the benches, and along the aisle, and under my table, and everywhere! I did not keep on—I had changed my mind, or rather had lost it, and found myself standing bewildered and silent, the thread of my discourse gone. A good-humored miner winked at me in a way that said, "They were too much for you." The dogs were finally ejected. The last I saw of them they were rolling down the hill, still fighting savagely. I resumed my discourse, and finished amid a steady but subdued a-a-a-a-a-h! of the quartette of babies. It is astonishing how long a delicate baby can keep up this sort of crying, and never get hoarse.

There were such strong signs of a storm one Wednesday afternoon, that I almost abandoned the idea of filling my appointment on Mormon Creek. The clouds were boiling up around the crests of the mountains, and the wind blew in heavy gusts. But, mounting the famous iron-gray pacing pony, I felt equal to any emergency, and at a rapid gait climbed the great hill dividing Sonora from Shaw's Flat, and passing a gap in Table Mountain, was soon dashing along the creek, facing a high wind, and exhilarated by the exercise. My miners were out in force, and I was glad I had not disappointed them. It is best in such doubtful cases *to go.*

By the time the service was over, the weather was still more portentous. The heavens were covered with thick clouds, and the wind had risen to a gale.

"You can never find your way home such a night as this," said a friendly miner. "You can't see your hand before you."

It was true—the darkness was so dense that not the faintest outline of my hand was visible an inch from my face. But I had confidence in the lively gray pony, and resolved to go home, having left the mistress of the parsonage alone in the little cabin which stood unfenced on the hill-side, and unprotected by lock or key to the doors. Mounting, I touched the pony gently with the whip, and he struck off at a lively pace up the road which led along the creek. I had confidence in the pony, and the pony seemed to have confidence in me. It was riding by faith, not by sight; I could not see even the pony's neck—the darkness was complete. I always feel a peculiar elation on horseback, and delighted with the rapid speed we were making, I was congratulating myself that I would not be long in getting home, when—horror! I felt that horse and rider were falling through the air. The pony had blindly paced right over the embankment, no more able to see than I was. Quick as thought I drew my feet out of the stirrups, and went headlong over the horse's head. Striking on my hands and knees, I was stunned at first, but soon found that beyond a few bruises and scratches I was not much hurt, though my watch was shattered. Getting on my feet, I listened for the pony, but in vain. Nothing could be heard or seen. Groping around a little, I stumbled into the creek. Erebus could not be darker than was that night. Having no notion of the points of the compass, I knew not which way to move. Long and loud I called for help, and at length, when I had almost exhausted myself, an answer came through the darkness, and soon a party appeared with a lantern. They found me on the edge of the creek, and the pony about midway down the embankment, where he had lodged in his fall, bracing himself with his fore feet, afraid to move. With great difficulty the poor beast, which was trembling in every limb with fright, was rescued from his perilous and uncomfortable position, and the whole party marched back to Jamison's. The pony was lamed in the fore shoulder, and my hands and knees were bleeding.

Taking a small hand-lantern with half a candle, and an umbrella, I started for Sonora on foot, leaving the pony in the corral. The rain began to fall just as I began to ascend the trail leading up the mountain, and the wind howled fearfully. A particularly heavy gust caught my umbrella at a disadvantage and tore it into shreds, and I threw it away and manfully took the rain which now poured in torrents, mingled with hail. Saturated as I was, the exercise kept me warm. My chief anxiety was to prevent my candle from being put out by the wind, of which the risk seemed great. But I protected my lantern with the skirt of my coat, while I watched carefully for the narrow trail. Winding around the ascent, jumping the mining ditches, and dripping with the rain, I reached the crossing of Table Mountain, and began picking my way among the huge lava-blocks on the summit. The storm struck me here unobstructed, and it seemed as if I would be actually blown away. The storm-king of the Sierras was on a big frolic that night! I soon lost the narrow trail. My piece of candle was burning low—if it should go out! A text came into my mind from which I preached the next Sunday: "*Walk while ye have the light.*" It was strange that the whole structure of the discourse shaped itself in my mind while stumbling among those rugged lava-blocks, and pelted by the storm which seemed every moment to rage more furiously. I kept groping for the lost trail, shivering now with cold, and the candle getting very low in my lantern. I was lost, and it was a bad night to be lost in. The wind seemed to have a mocking sound as it shrieked in my ears, and as it died away in a temporary lull it sounded like a dirge. I began to think it would have been better for me to have taken the advice of my Mormon Creek friends and waited until morning. All the time I kept moving, though aimlessly. Thank God, here is the trail! I came upon it again just where it left the mountain and crossed the Jamestown road, recognizing the place by a gap in a brush fence. I started forward at a quickened pace, following the trail among the manzanita bushes, and winding among the hills. A tree had fallen across the trail at one point, and in going round it I lost the little thread of pathway and could not find it again. The earth was flooded with water, and one spot looked just like another. Holding my lantern near the ground, I scanned keenly every foot of ground as I made a circle in search of the lost trail, but soon found I had no idea of the points of the compass—in a word, I was lost again. The storm was unabated. It was rough work stumbling over the rocks and pushing my way through the thick manzanita bushes, bruising my limbs and scratching my face.

Almost exhausted, I sat down on the lee side of a large pine-tree, thinking I would thus wait for daylight. But the next moment the thought occurred to me that if I sat there much longer I would never leave alive, for I was getting very cold, and would freeze before morning. I thought it was time to pray, and I prayed. A strange, sweet calm came over me, and rising, I resumed my search for the lost trail. In five minutes I found it, and following it, I soon came in sight of a light which issued from a cabin, at the door of which I knocked. At first there was no answer, and I repeated the thumps on the door with more energy. I heard whispering inside, a step across the floor, then the latch was drawn, and as the door was partially opened a gruff voice said—

"Who are you? and what do you want here at this time o' night?"

"Let me in out of the storm, and I will tell you," I said.

"Not so fast, stranger—robbers are mighty plenty and sassy round here, and you do n't come in 'til we know who you are," said the voice.

I told them who I was, where I had been, and all about it. The door was opened cautiously, and I walked in. A coarse, frowzy-looking woman sat in the corner by the fire-place, a rough-looking man sat in the opposite corner, while the fellow who had let me in took a seat on a bench in front. I stood dripping, and ready to sink from fatigue, but no seat was offered me.

"This is a pretty rough night," said one of the men, complacently; "but it's nothing to the night we had the storm on the plains, when our wagon-covers was blowed off, and the cattle stampeded, and"—

"Stop!" said I, "your troubles are over, and mine are not. I want you to give me a piece of candle for my lantern here, and tell me the way to Sonora."

The fact is, I was disgusted at their want of hospitality, and too tired to be polite. It is vain to expect much politeness from a man who is very tired or very hungry. Most wives find this out, but I mention it for the sake of the young and inexperienced.

After considerable delay, the frowzy woman got up, found a candle, cut off about three inches, and sulkily handed it to me. Lighting and placing it in my lantern, I made for the door, receiving these directions as I did so:

"Go back the way you came about two hundred yards, then take a left-hand trail, which will carry you to Sonora by way of Dragoon Gulch."

Plunging into the storm again, I found the trail as directed, and went forward. The rain poured

4

down as if the bottom of the heavens had fallen out, and the earth was a sea, the water coming above my gaiters at every step, and the wind almost lifting me from my feet. I soon found that it was impossible to distinguish the trail, and trusting to my instinct I pressed on in the direction of Sonora, which could scarcely be more than a mile away. Seeing a light in the distance, I bent my steps toward it. In my eagerness to reach it I came very near walking into a deep mining shaft—a single step more, and this sketch would never have been written. Making my way among huge bowlders and mining pits, I reached the house in which was the light I had followed. Knocking at the door, a cheerful voice said, "Come in." Pushing open the door, I entered, and found that I was in a drinking-saloon. Several men were seated around a table playing cards, with money piled before them, and glasses of strong drink within reach. A red-faced, corpulent, and good-natured Dutchman stood behind the bar, and was in the act of mixing some stimulant with the flourish of an expert.

"Where am I?" I asked, thoroughly bewildered, and not recognizing the place or the persons before me.

"Dis is de Shaw's Flat Lager-beer Saloon," said the Dutchman.

So this was not Sonora: after losing the trail I

had lost my course, and gone away off north of my intended destination. The men knew me, and were very polite. The kind-hearted Dutchman offered me alcoholic refreshment, which I politely declined, placed a whole candle in my lantern, and gave me many good wishes as I again took the road and faced the storm. Gambling is a terrible vice, but it was a good thing for me that the card-players lingered so long at their sport that rough night. Taking the middle of the road, I struck a good pace, and meeting with no farther mishap except a fall and tumble in the red mud as I was descending the high hill that separated the two camps, about two o'clock in the morning I came in sight of the parsonage, and saw an anxious face at the door looking out into the darkness.

After a sound sleep, I rose next day a little bruised and stiff, but otherwise none the worse for being lost on Table Mountain. The gallant gray pony did not escape so well; he never did get over his lameness.

FULTON.

HE was a singular compound—hero, hypochondriac, and saint.

He came aboard the *Antelope* as we (wife and I) were on our way to the Annual Conference at Sacramento, in 1855. Coming into our state-room, he introduced himself as "Brother Fulton." A thin, pale-faced man, with weak blue eyes, and that peculiar look which belongs to the real ascetic, he looked out of place among that motley throng.

"I am glad to see you, and hope you will live holy and be useful in California," he said.

"As this is the first time we have ever met," he continued, "let us have a word of prayer, that all our intercourse may be sanctified to our mutual good."

Down he kneeled among the trunks, valises, and bandboxes in the little state-room (and we with him, though it was tight squeezing amid the baggage), and prayed long and fervently, with many groans and sighs.

Rising at length from our knees, we entered into conversation. After a few inquiries and answers, he said—

"It is very difficult to maintain a spiritual frame of mind among all these people. Let us have another word of prayer."

Down he went again on his knees, we following, and he wrestled long and earnestly in supplication, oblivious of the peculiarities of the situation.

Conversation was resumed on rising, confined exclusively to religious topics. A few minutes had thus been spent, when he said—

"We are on our way to the Annual Conference, where we shall be engaged in looking after the interests of the Church. Let us have another word of prayer, that we may be prepared for these duties, and that the session may be profitable to all."

Again he knelt upon his knees and prayed with great fervor.

When we rose there was a look of inquiry in the eyes of my fellow-missionary, which seemed to ask, Where is this to end?

Just then the dinner-bell rang, and we had no opportunity for farther devotions with Brother Fulton just then.

It was observed during the Conference session

that there was a cloud in Fulton's sky—he sat silent and gloomy, taking no part in the proceedings. About the third morning, while some important measure was pending, he rose and addressed Bishop Andrew, who was in the chair—

"Bishop, I am in great mental distress; you will excuse me for interrupting the business of the Conference, but I can bear it no longer."

"What's the matter, Brother Fulton?" asked that bluff, wise old prelate.

"I am afraid I have sinned," was the answer, with bowed head and faltering voice.

"In what way?" asked the Bishop.

"I will explain: On my way from the mountains I became very hungry in the stage-coach. I am afraid I thought too much of my food. You know, Bishop, that if we fix our affections for one moment on any creature more than on God, it is sin."

"Well, Brother Fulton," said the Bishop, "if at your hungriest moment the alternative had been presented whether you should give up your God or your dinner, would you have hesitated?"

"No, sir," said Brother Fulton meekly, after a short pause.

"Well, then, my dear brother, the case is clear, you have done no wrong," said the Bishop in his hearty, off-hand way.

The effect was magical. Fulton stood thoughtful a moment, and then, as he sat down, burst into tears of joy. Poor, morbidly-sensitive soul! we may smile at such scruples, so foreign to the temper of these after-times, but they were the scruples of a soul as true and as unworldly as that of á Kempis.

He was sent to the mines, and he was a wonder to those nomadic dwellers about Vallecito, Douglass's Flat, Murphy's Camp, and Lancha Plana. They were puzzled to determine whether he was a lunatic or a saint. Many stories of his eccentricities were afloat, and he was regarded with a sort of mingled curiosity and awe. It was but seldom that even the roughest fellows would utter profane language in his presence, and when they did, they received a rebuke that made them ashamed. Before the year was out he had won every heart by the power of simple truthfulness, courage, and goodness. The man who insulted, or in any way mistreated him, would have lost caste with those wild adventurers who, with all their grievous faults, never failed to recognize sincerity and pluck. Fulton's sincerity was unmistakable, and he feared not the face of man. He made converts among them, too. Many a profane lip became familiar with the language of prayer in those mining camps where the devil was so terribly regnant, and took no pains to hide his cloven foot.

One of Fulton's eccentricities caused a tedious trial to an old hen belonging to a good sister at Vallecito. He was a dyspeptic—too great abstemiousness the cause. His diet was tea, crackers, and boiled eggs. Being a rigid Sabbath-keeper, he would eat nothing cooked on Sunday. So his eggs were boiled on Saturday, and warmed over for his Sunday meals. About the time of one of his visits to Vallecito, the sister referred to had occasion to set a hen. The period of incubation was singularly protracted, running far into the summer. The eggs would not hatch. Investigation finally disclosed the fact that by somebody's blunder the boiled eggs had been placed under the unfortunate fowl, whose perseverance failed of its due reward. "Bless me!" said the good-natured sister, laughing, "these were Brother Fulton's eggs. I wonder if he ate the raw ones?"

Fulton had his stated times for private devotion, and allowed nothing to stand in the way. The hour of twelve was one of these seasons sacred to prayer. One day he was ascending a mountain, leading his horse, and assisting a teamster by scotching the wheels of his heavy wagon when his horses stopped to get breath. When about half way up, Fulton's large, old-fashioned silver watch told him it was twelve. Instantly he called out—

Fulton. 57

"My hour for prayer has arrived, and I must stop and pray."

"Wait 'til we get to the top of the mountain, won't you?" exclaimed the teamster.

"No," said Fulton, "I never allow any thing to interfere with my secret prayers."

And down he kneeled by the roadside, bridle in hand, and with closed eyes he was soon wrapt in devotion.

The teamster expressed his view of the situation in language not exactly congruous to the exercise in which his fellow-traveler was engaged. But he waited until the prayer was ended, and then with a serene face Fulton resumed his service as scotcher, and the summit was reached in triumph.

While on the San Ramon Circuit, in Contra Costa county, he met a man with a drove of hogs in a narrow, muddy lane. The swine took fright, and despite the frantic efforts of their driver, they turned, bolted by him, and rushed back the way whence they had come. The swine-herd was furious with rage, and let loose upon Fulton a volley of oaths and threats. Fulton paused, looked upon the angry fellow calmly for a few moments, and then dismounted, and kneeling by the roadside, began to pray for the man whose profanity was filling the air. The fellow was confounded at the sight of that ghostly-looking man on his knees before him; he took a panic, and turning back, he followed his hogs in rapid flight. The sequel must be given. The fleeing swine-herd became one of Fulton's converts, dating his religious concern from the prayer in the lane.

Fulton itinerated in this way for years, fasting rigidly and praying incessantly, some thinking him a lunatic, others reverencing him as a saint. Thinner and thinner did he grow, his pallid face becoming almost transparent. Thinking its mild climate might benefit his health, he was sent to Southern California. One morning, on entering his room, he was found kneeling by his bedside dead, with his Bible open before him, and a smile on his face.

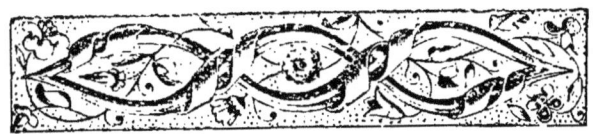

BLIGHTED.

ALCOHOL and opium were his masters. He alternated in their use. Only a brain of extraordinary strength, and nerves of steel, could have stood the strain. He had a large practice at the Sonora bar, was a popular politician, made telling stump speeches, and wrote pungent and witty editorials for the *Union Democrat,* conducted by that most genial and unselfish of party pack-horses, A. N. Francisco. He was a fine scholar, and so thoroughly a gentleman in his instincts that even when drunk he was not vulgar or obscene. Cynicism and waggery were mingled in his nature, but he was more cynic than wag. An accidental meeting under pleasant circumstances, and agreement in opinion concerning certain current issues that were exciting the country, developed a sort of friendship between us. He affected skepticism, and was always ready to give a thrust at the clergy. It sometimes happened that a party of the wild blades of the place would come in a body to my little church on the hill-side, to hear such a discourse as my immaturity could furnish, but he was never among them. All he seemed to want from the community in which he lived was something to sneer or laugh at, and the means wherewith to procure the narcotics with which he was destroying his body and brain. As we met oftener, I became interested in him more and more. Looking at his splendid head and handsome face, it was impossible not to admire him and think of the possibilities of his life could he be freed from his vices. He was still under thirty. But he was a drunkard.

He was shy of all allusions to himself, and I do not know how it was that he came to open his mind to me so freely as he did one morning. I found him alone in his office. He was sober and sad, and in a different mood from any in which I had ever before met him. Our conversation touched upon many topics, for he seemed disposed to talk.

"How slight a circumstance," I remarked, "will sometimes give coloring to our whole character, and affect all our after-life!"

"Yes," he answered, "bitterly do I realize the truth of your remark. When I was in my fourteenth year an incident occurred which has influenced all my subsequent life. I was always a favorite with my school-teachers, and I loved them with

Blighted. 61

a hearty boyish affection. Especially did I entertain a most affectionate reverence for the kind old man who presided over the boys' academy in my native town in Massachusetts. He became my instructor when I was ten years old, and I was his favorite pupil. With a natural aptness for study, my desire to win his approbation stimulated me to make exertions that always kept me at the head of my class, and I was frequently held up to the other pupils as an example of good behavior. I was proud of his good opinion, and sought to deserve it. Stimulated both by ambition and affection, nothing seemed too difficult for me. The three years I was under his tuition were the best employed and happiest of my life. But my kind old preceptor died. The whole town was plunged in deep sorrow for his loss, and my boyish grief was bitter."

Here he paused a few moments, and then went on:—

"Soon a new teacher took his place. He was unlike the one we had lost. He was a younger man, and he lacked the gentleness and dignity of his predecessor. But I was prepared to give him my confidence and affection, for then I had learned nothing else. I sought to gain his favor, and was diligent in study and careful of my behavior. For several days all went on smoothly. A rule of the school forbade whispering. One day a boy sitting just behind me whispered my name. Involuntarily, I half inclined my head toward him, when the new teacher called to me angrily—

"'Come here, sir!'

"I obeyed. Grasping me tightly by the collar, he said:

"'How dare you whisper in school?'

"I told him I had not whispered. 'Hearing my name called, I only turned to'—

"'Don't dare to tell me a lie!' he thundered, lifting me from the floor as he spoke, and tripping my feet from under me, causing me to fall violently, my head striking first.

"I was stunned by the fall, but soon rose to my feet, bruised and bewildered, yet burning with indignation.

"'Take your seat, sir!' said he—enforcing the command by several sharp strokes of the rod—'and be careful in future how you lie to me!'

"I walked slowly to my seat. A demon had entered my soul. For the first time I had learned to hate. I hated that man from that hour, and I hate him still! He still lives, and if I ever meet him, I will be even with him yet!"

He had unconsciously risen from his seat, while his eyes flashed, and his face was distorted with passion. After a few moments, he continued:

Blighted. 63

"This affair produced a complete change in my conduct and character. I hated my teacher. I looked upon him as an enemy, and treated him accordingly. Losing all relish for study, from being at the head I dropped to the foot of my class. Instead of seeking to merit a name for good behavior, my only ambition was to annoy the tyrant placed over me. He treated me harshly, and I suffered severely. He beat me constantly and cruelly. Under these influences my nature hardened rapidly. I received no sympathy except from my mother, and she did not understand my position. I felt that *she* loved me, though she evidently thought I must be in the wrong. My father laid all the blame on me, and, with a stern sense of justice, refused to interfere in my behalf. At last I began to look upon him as the accomplice of my persecutor, and almost hated him too. I became suspicious and misanthropic. I loved no one but my mother, and sought the love of no other. Thus passed several years. My time was wasted, and my nature perverted. I was sent to college, for which I was but poorly prepared. Here a new life begun. My effort to rise above the influences that had been so hurtful to me failed. My college career soon terminated. I could not shake off the effects of the early injustice and mismanagement of which I was the victim. I came to California in a reckless spirit, and am now mortgaged to the devil. What I might have been under other circumstances, I know not; but I do know that the best elements of my nature were crushed out of me by the infernal tyrant who was my teacher, and that I owe him a debt I would be glad to pay."

He spoke truly. The mortgage was duly foreclosed. He died of *delirium tremens*. A single act of injustice sowed the seeds of bitterness that marred the hopes of a whole life. The moral of this sketch is commended to teachers and parents.

STRANDED.

JUST as the sun was going down, after one of the hottest days of the summer of 1855, while we were seated in the rude piazza of the parsonage in Sonora, enjoying the coolness of the evening breeze, a man in his shirt sleeves came up, and in a hurried tone inquired—

"Does the preacher live here?"

Getting an affirmative answer, he said—

"There is a very sick man at the hospital who wishes to see the Southern Methodist preacher immediately."

I at once obeyed the summons. On reaching the hospital, my conductor said—

"You will find him in there," pointing to one of the rooms.

On entering, I found four patients in the room, three of whom were young men, variously affected with chronic diseases—rough-looking fellows, showing plainly in their sensual faces the insignia of vice. The fourth was a man perhaps fifty years old. As he lay there in the light of the setting sun, I thought I had never beheld a more ghastly object. The death-like pallor, the pinched features, the unnatural gleam of his eyes in their sunken sockets, telling of days of pain, and nights without sleep—all told me this was the man by whom I had been sent for.

"Are you the preacher?" he asked in a feeble voice, as I approached the bedside.

"Yes; I am the preacher. Can I do any thing for you?"

"I am glad you have come—I was afraid I would not get to see you. Take a seat on that stool—the accommodations are rather poor here."

He paused to recover breath, and then went on:

"I want you to pray for me. I was once a member of the Methodist Church, in Georgia; but O sir, I have been a bad man in California—a wicked, wicked wretch! I have a family in Georgia—a dear wife and "—

Here he broke down again.

"I had hoped to see them once more, but the doctors say I must die, and I feel that I am sinking. No tongue could tell what I have suffered, but the worst of all is my shameful denial of my Saviour. What a fool I have been, to think that I could prosper in sin! Here I am, stranded, wrecked, by my own folly. I have been here in the hospital two months, and have suffered intensely all the time. What a fool I have been! Will you pray for me?"

After directing his attention to various passages of the Bible expressive of the infinite and tender love of God toward the erring, I kneeled by his cot and prayed. His sighs and sobs gave indication of deep feeling, and when I arose from my knees the tears were running from his eyes, and his face wore a different expression.

"Return unto me, and I will return unto you," he said, repeating the words which I had quoted from the word of God—"return unto me, and I will return unto you"—lingering upon the words with peculiar satisfaction. He seemed to have caught a great truth.

I continued my visits to him for several weeks. He gave me the history of his life, which had been one of vicissitude and adventure. He had been a soldier in the Seminole war in Florida, and he had much to say of alligators, and Indians, and Andrew Jackson. All the time his strength was failing, his eyes glittering more intensely. His bodily sufferings were frightful; the only sleep he obtained was by the use of opiates. But an extraordinary change had taken place in his mental state. To say that he was happy would be putting it too tamely. There was some unseen Presence or Power that lifted his soul above his suffering body, making that lonely room all bright and peaceful. What it was, no true believer in the Saviour and lover of our souls will doubt.

"There's a great change in the old man," said the nurse one day; "he doesn't fret at all now."

"O I have been so happy all night and all day!" he said to me the last time I saw him. "I have only refrained from shouting for fear of disturbing these poor fellows, my sick room-mates. I have felt all day as if I could take them all in my arms, and fly with them to the skies!" And his face was radiant.

The next morning he was found on the floor by his bedside—dead. He had died so quietly that none knew it. His papers were placed in my possession. In his well-worn pocket-book, among letters from his wife in Georgia, receipts, and private papers of various kinds, I found the following lines, which he had clipped from some newspaper, and which seemed tear-blotted:

COME HOME, PAPA!

(*A little girl's thoughts about her absent father.*)

Come home, papa! the shades of night
  Are gathering in the sky;
The fire-fly shines with fitful light,
  The stars are out on high,

Stranded.

And twinkles bright the evening star:
We have waited long—come home, papa!

Come home! the birds have gone to rest
   In many a forest tree;
Within thy quiet home, thy nest,
   Thy bird is waiting thee;
She softly sings, to cheer mamma,
The while she waits—come home, papa!

Come home! A tear is glistening bright
   Within my mother's eye;
Why stay away so late to-night
   From home, mamma, and I?
"Alas!" "alas!" her moanings are
That thou canst not return, papa!

She says the white-sailed ship hath borne
   Thee far upon the sea,
That many a night and many a morn
   Will pass nor bring us thee;
But bear thee from us swift and far,
And thou mayst not come home, papa!

I thought thou wouldst return when light
   Had faded on the sea:
How can I fall asleep to-night
   Without a kiss from thee?
Thy picture in my hand I hold,
But O the lips are hard and cold!

Come home! I'm sad where'er I go,
   To find no father there:
How can we live without thee so?
   I'll say my evening prayer,

And ask the God who made each star,
To bring me home my dear papa!

ANSWERED.

I'll come! I'll come! my darling one,
    Though long from thee I've tarried.
For thee within my anxious breast
    The fondest love I've carried
Where'er I've roamed o'er land or sea.
Be not dismayed, I'll come to thee.

When evening shades around thee fall,
    And birds have gone to rest,
O sing, thou sweetest bird of mine,
    Within thy lonely nest!
Sing on! sing on! to cheer "mamma"
"The while she waits" for thy "papa."

O tell thy mother not to weep,
    But let her tears be dry,
And ne'er for me to let them creep
    Into her cheerful eye;
For though I've strayed from her afar,
She soon shall welcome home "papa."

Though "white-sailed ship" hath borne me far
    Across the restless sea—
Though many nights and morns have passed
    Since last I dwelt with thee—
Yet, lovely one, I tell thee true,
But death can sever me from you.

O lay that picture down, sweet child,
    And calmly rest in sleep,
And for my absence long from thee
    I pray thee not to weep!

Stranded. 71

I'll come! I'll come again to thee,
In "white-sailed ship" across the sea.

But no "white-sailed ship" ever bore him to the loved ones across the sea. He sleeps on one of the red hills overlooking Sonora, awaiting the resurrection.

As these are not fancy sketches, but simple recitals of actual California life, the lines above were copied as found; the friendly reader therefore will not judge them with critical severity.

LOCKLEY.

HE was eccentric, and he was lazy — very eccentric, and very lazy. The miners crowded his church on Sundays, and he moved around among them in a leisurely, familiar way, during the week, saying the quaintest things, eating their slap-jacks, and smoking their best cigars. He occupied a little frame house near the church in Columbia, then the richest mining camp in the world, in whose streets ten thousand miners lounged, ate, drank, gambled, quarreled, and fought every Lord's-day. That bachelor parsonage was unique in respect of the furniture it did not contain, and also in respect to the condition of that which it did contain. Lockley was not a neat house-keeper. I have said he was lazy. He knew the fact, accepted it, and gloried in it. On one occasion he invited four friends to supper. They all arrived at the hour. Lockley was stretched at full length on a lounge which would have been better for the attention of an upholsterer or washerwoman. The friends looked at each other, and at their host. One of them spoke—

"Lockley, where's your supper?"

"O it isn't cooked yet," he drawled out.

"Parker," continued Lockley, "make a fire in that stove. Toman, you go up town and get some crackers, and oysters, and coffee, and a steak. Oxley, go after a bucket of water. Porterfield, you hunt up the crockery, and set the table."

His orders were obeyed by the amused guests, who entered into the spirit of the occasion with great good humor. Oyster cans were opened, the steak was duly sliced, seasoned, and broiled, the coffee was boiled, and in due time the supper was ready, and Lockley arose from the lounge and presided at the table with perfect enjoyment.

Two of these guests had a tragic history. Oxley and Parker were killed in Mexico, at the massacre of the Crabb party. Porterfield died in Stockton. Toman, I think, lives somewhere in Indiana.

I saw one of Lockley's letters from Los Angeles, whither he had been sent by Bishop Andrew, in 1855. It was as follows:

LOS ANGELES, August, 1855.

Dear Porterfield:—I have been here six months. There are three Protestant churches in the place. Their united congregations amount to ten persons. My receipts from collections during six months amount to ten dollars. I have been studying a great scientific question, namely, the location of the seat of hunger. Is it in the stomach, or in the brain? After consulting all the best authorities, *and no little experience,* I have concluded that it is migratory—first in one, and then in the other! Take care of my cats.

             LOCKLEY.

 I had a letter from him once. It was in reply to one from me asking him to remit the amount of a bill he owed for books. As it was brief, I print it entire:

          MARIPOSA, April, 1858.

 *Dear Fitz:—*Your dunning letter has been received and —placed on file.   Yours,   E. B. LOCKLEY.

 The first time I ever heard him preach was at San Jose, during a special meeting. Poising himself in his peculiar way, with an expression half comic, half serious, he began: "I have a notion, my friends, that in a gospel land every man has his own preacher—that is, for every man there is some one preacher, who, from similarity of temperament and mental constitution, is adapted to be the instrument of his salvation. Now," he continued, "there may be some man in this audience so peculiar, so cranky, so much out of the common order, *that I am his man.* If so, may the Holy Spirit send the truth to his heart!" This remark riveted attention, and he held it to the close.

 Lazy as he was out of the pulpit, in it he was all energy and fire. He had read largely, had a good memory, and put the quaintest conceits into the quaintest setting of fitting words. His favorite text was, "There remaineth a rest to the people of God." That was his idea of heaven—rest to "sit down" with Abraham, Isaac, and Jacob, in the kingdom of God. On this theme he was indeed eloquent. The rapturous songs, the waving palms, the sounding harps of the New Jerusalem, were not to his taste—what he wanted, and looked for, was rest, and all the images by which he described the felicity of the redeemed were drawn from that one thought. His idea of hell was antithetic to this. The terrible thought with him was, that there was no rest there. I heard him bring out this idea with awful power one Sunday morning at Linden, in San Joaquin county. "In this world," said Lockley, "there is respite from every grief, every burden, every pain in the body. The mourner weeps herself to sleep. The agony of pain sinks exhausted into slumber. Sleep, sweet sleep, brings surcease to all human griefs and pains in this life. *But there will be no sleep in hell!* The accusing conscience will hiss its reproaches into the ear of the lost, the memory will reproduce the crimes and follies by which the soul was wrecked forever, the fires of retribution will burn on unintermittingly. One hour of sleep in a thousand years would be some mitigation—but the worm dieth not, the fire is not quenched. God deliver me from a sleepless hell!" he exclaimed, his swarthy face glowing, and his dark eye gleaming, his whole frame quivering with horror at the thought his mind had conceived.

He was original in the pulpit, as everywhere else. At one time the preachers of the Pacific Conference seemed to have a sort of epidemic of preaching on a certain topic—*The Choice of Moses.* The elders preached it at the quarterly meetings, and it was carried around from circuit to circuit, and from station to station. There was not much variety in these sermons. They all bore a generic likeness to each other, indicating a common paternity, at least, for the outlines. The matter had become a subject of pleasant banter among the brethren. There was consequently some surprise, when at the session of the Annual Conference, Lockley announced for his text: "Moses chose rather to suffer affliction with the people of God, than to enjoy the pleasures of sin for a season." It was the old text, but it was a new sermon. The choice of Moses was, in his hands, a topic fresh and entertaining, as he threw upon it the flashes of his wit, and evoked from it suggestions that never would have occurred to another mind. "Mind you," he said at one point, "Moses chose to suffer affliction *with the people of God.* I tell you, my brethren, the people of God are sometimes very aggravating. They fretted Moses almost to death. But did he forsake them? Did he leave them in the wilderness to perish in their foolishness? No—he stood by them to the last." His application of this peculiar exegesis to the audience of preachers and Church-members was so pointed that the ripple of amusement that swept over their faces gave way to an expression of seriousness that told that the shot had hit the mark.

One warm day in 1858 he started out with me to make a canvass of the city of Stockton for the Church-paper. We kept in pretty brisk motion for an hour or two, Lockley giving an occasional sign of dissatisfaction at the unwonted activity into which he had been beguiled. Passing down Weber Avenue, on the shady side of a corner store he saw an empty chair, and with a sigh of relief he sank into it.

"Come on, Lockley," said I; "we are not half done our work."

"I sha'n't do it," he drawled.

"Why not?" I asked.

"The Scripture is against it," he answered with great seriousness of tone.

"How is that?" I asked with curiosity.

"The Scripture says, 'Do thyself no harm,'" said he, "and it does me harm to walk as fast as you do. I sha'n't budge."

Nor did he. I spent two or three hours in different parts of the city, and on my return found him sitting in exactly the same attitude in which I had left him, a picture of perfect contentment. Literally, he had n't budged.

While on the Santa Clara Circuit he drove a remarkable little sorrel mare named by him Ginsy. Ginsy was very small, very angular, with long fetlocks and mane a shade lighter than her other parts, a short tail that had a comic sort of twist to one side, and a lame eye. The buggy was in keeping with Ginsy. It was battered and splintered, some of the spokes were new and some were old, the dash-board was a wreck, the wheels seesawed in a curious way as it moved. And the harness!—it was too much for my powers. It was a conglomerate harness, composed of leather, hay rope, fragments of suspenders, whip-cord, and rawhide. The vehicle announced its approach by an extraordinary creaking of all its unoiled axles, a sort of calliopean quartette that regaled the ears of the fat and happy genius who held the reins. Lockley, Ginsy, and that buggy, made a picture worth looking at.

While Lockley was on this circuit the Annual Conference was held at San Jose. As Bishop Kavanaugh was to preach on Sunday morning, it was expected that an overwhelming congregation would crowd the San Jose church, that eloquent Kentuckian being a favorite with all classes in California. Lockley asked that a preacher be sent to fill the pulpit of his little church in the town of Santa Clara, three miles distant. The genial and zealous James Kelsay was sent. At eleven o'clock he and Lockley entered the church, and ascended the pulpit. After kneeling a few moments in the usual way, they seated themselves and faced the—not the audience, for none was there. Nobody had come. In a few minutes an old man came in and took a seat in the farthest corner from the pulpit. He eyed the two preachers, and they eyed him in silence. The minutes passed on. There they sat. As might have been expected, everybody had gone to hear the Bishop, in San Jose. That old man was the only person who entered the church. It was evident, however, that he had come to stay. He rigidly kept his place, never taking his eyes from the two preachers, who repaid him with an attention equally fixed. A pin might have been heard to drop—not a sound was uttered as they thus sat and gazed at each other. An hour passed, and still they sat speechless. Lockley broke the silence. Turning to his companion in the pulpit, he said gravely—

"*Brother Kelsay, how shall we bring these solemn services to a close?*"

"Let us pray," said Kelsay.

They kneeled, and Kelsay led in prayer, the old man keeping his place and sitting position. The benediction was then formally pronounced, and that service ended.

His death was tragic and pitiful. A boy, standing in the sunken channel of a dry creek, shot at a vicious dog on the bank above. The bullet, after striking and killing the dog, struck Lockley in the chest as he was approaching the spot. He staggered backward to a fence close at hand, fell on his knees, and died praying.

FATHER COX.

FATHER COX was a physical and intellectual phenomenon. He was of immense girth, weighing more than three hundred pounds. His face was ruddy and almost as smooth as that of a child, his hair snow-white and fine as floss-silk, his eyes a deep blue, his features small. His great size, and the contrast between the infantile freshness of his skin and white hair, made him a notable man in the largest crowd.

He was converted, and joined the Methodist Church, after he had passed his fiftieth year. He had been, as he himself phrased it, the keeper of a "doggery," and was no doubt a rough customer. Reaching California by way of Texas, he at once began to preach. His style took with the Californians; great crowds flocked to hear him, and marvelous effects were produced. He was a fine judge of human nature, and knew the direct way to the popular heart. Under his preaching men wept, prayed, repented, believed, and flocked into the Church by scores and hundreds.

Father Cox was in his glory at a camp-meeting. To his gift of exhortation was added that of song. He had a voice like a flute in its softness and purity of tone, and his solos before and after preaching melted and broke the hard heart of many a wild and reckless Californian.

His sagacity and knowledge of human nature were exhibited at one of his camp-meetings held at Gilroy, in Santa Clara county. There was a great crowd and a great religious excitement, Father Cox riding its topmost wave, the general of the army of Israel. Seated in the preachers' stand, he was leading in one of the spirited lyrics suited to the occasion, when a young man approached him and said—

"Father Cox, there's a friend of mine out here who wants you to come and pray for him."

"Where is he?"

"Just out there on the edge of the crowd," answered the young fellow.

Father Cox followed him to the outskirts of the congregation, where he found a group of rough-looking fellows standing around, with their leggings and huge Spanish spurs, in the center of which a man was seen kneeling, with his face buried between his hands.

"There he is," said the guide.

"Is he a friend of yours, gentlemen?" asked Father Cox, turning to the expectant group.

"Yes," answered one of them.

"And you want me to pray for him, do you?" he continued.

"We do," was the answer.

"All right—all of you kneel down, and I'll pray for him."

They looked at one another in confusion, and then one by one they sheepishly kneeled until all were down.

Father Cox then kneeled down by the "mourner," and prayed as follows:

"O Lord, thou knowest all things. Thou knowest whether this man is a sincere penitent or not. If he is sincerely sorry for his sins, and is bowing before Thee with a broken heart and a contrite spirit, have mercy upon him, hear his prayer, pardon his transgressions, give him Thy peace, and make him Thy child. But, O Lord, if he is not in earnest, if he is here as an emissary of Satan, to make mockery of sacred things, and to hinder Thy work, kill him—kill him, Lord"—

At this point the "mourner" became frightened, and began to crawl, Father Cox following him on his knees, and continuing his prayer. The terror-stricken sinner could stand it no longer, but sprang to his feet, and bounded away at full speed, leaving Father Cox master of the field, while the kneeling roughs rose and sneaked off abashed and discomfited.

The sequel of this incident should be given. The mock penitent was taken into the Church by Father Cox soon after. He left the camp-ground in a state of great alarm on account of his sacrilegious frolic.

"When the old man put his hand on me as I knelt there in wicked sport, and prayed as he did, it seemed to me that I felt hot flashes from hell rise in my face," said he; "right there I became a true penitent."

The man thus strangely converted became a faithful soldier of the cross.

At a camp-meeting near the town of Sonoma, in 1858, Father Cox, who was preacher in charge of that circuit, rose to exhort after the venerable Judge Shattuck had preached one of his strong, earnest sermons. The meeting had been going on several days, and the Sonoma sinners had hitherto resisted all appeals and persuasions. The crowd was great, and every eye was fixed upon the old man as he began his exhortation.

"Boys," he began, in a familiar, kindly way, "boys, you are treating me badly. I have been with you all the year, and you have always had a kind word and a generous hand for the old man.

I love you, and I love your immortal souls. I have entreated you to turn away from your sins, to repent, and come to Christ and be saved. I have preached to you, I have prayed for you, I have wept over you. You harden your hearts, and stiffen your necks, and will not yield. You *will* be lost! You *will* go to hell! In the judgment-day you will be left without excuse. And boys," he continued, his mighty chest heaving, his voice quivering, and the tears running down his cheeks, "boys, I will have to be a witness against you. I shall have to testify that I warned, persuaded, and entreated you in vain. I shall have to testify of the proceedings of this Sabbath night, and tell how you turned a deaf ear to the call of your Saviour. I shall have to hear your sentence of condemnation, and see you driven down to hell. My God! the thought is dreadful! Spare me this agony. Don't, O don't force this upon me! Don't compel the old man to be a witness against you in that awful day! Rather," he continued, "hear my voice of invitation to-night, and come to Christ, so that instead of being a witness against you in that day, I may be able to present you as my spiritual children, and say, Lord Jesus, here is the old man, and his Sonoma children, all saved, and all ready to join together in a glad hallelujah to the Lamb that was slain!"

It was overwhelming. The pathos and power of the speaker were indescribable. There was a "break-down" all over the vast congregation, and a rush of penitents to the altar, as one of the stirring camp-meeting choruses pealed forth from the full hearts of the faithful.

Father Cox's ready wit was equal to any occasion. At a camp-meeting in the Bodega Hills, in "opening the doors of the Church," he said:

"Many souls have been converted, and now I want them all to join the Church. When I was a boy, I learned that it was best to string my fish as I caught them, lest they should flutter back into the water. I want to string my fish—that is, take all the young converts into the Church, and put them to work for Christ, lest they go back into the world"—

"You can't catch *me!*" loudly interrupted a rowdyish-looking fellow who sat on a slab near the rostrum.

"I am not fishing for *gar!*" retorted Father Cox, casting a contemptuous glance at the fellow, and then went on with his work.

The gar-fish is the abomination of all true fishermen—hard to catch, coarse-flavored, bony, and nearly worthless when caught. The vulgar fellow became the butt of the camp-ground, and soon mounted his mustang, and galloped off, amid the derision even of his own sort.

Father Cox had a naturally hot temper, which sometimes flamed forth in a way that was startling. It would have been a bold man who would have tested his physical prowess in a combat. Beside him an ordinary-sized person looked like a pigmy. Near San Juan, in Monterey county, he had occasion to cross a swollen stream by means of the water-fence above the ford. The fence was flimsy, and Father Cox was heavy. The undertaking was not an easy one at best, and Father Cox's difficulty and annoyance were enhanced by the ungenerous and violent abuse and curses of an infidel blacksmith on the opposite side of the stream, who had worked himself into a rage because the immense weight of the old man had broken a rail or two of the fence. The situation was too critical for reply, as the mammoth preacher Cox "cooned" his way cautiously and painfully across the rickety bridge, at the imminent risk every moment of tumbling headlong into the roaring torrent below. Meanwhile the wicked and angry blacksmith kept up a volley of oaths and insulting epithets. The old Adam was waking up in the old preacher. By the time he had reached the shore he was thoroughly mad, and rushing forward, he grasped his persecutor and shook him until his breath was nearly shaken out of him, saying—

"O you foul-mouthed villain! If it were not

for the fear of my God I would beat you into a jelly!"

The blacksmith, a stalwart fellow, was astonished; and when Father Cox let him go, he had a new view of the Church militant. This scene was witnessed by a number of bystanders, who did not fail to report it, and it made the old preacher a hero with the rough fellows of San Juan, who thenceforward flocked to hear his preaching as they did to hear nobody else.

The image of Father Cox that is most vivid to my mind as I close this unpretentious sketch, is that which he presented as he stood in the pulpit at Stockton one night, during the Conference session, and sang, "I am going home to die no more," his ruddy face aglow, his blue eyes swimming in tears, his white hair glistening in the lamp-light. He sleeps on the Bodega Hills, amid the oaks and madronas, whose branches wave in the breezes of the blue Pacific. He has gone home to die no more.

AN INTERVIEW.

AS I was coming out of the San Francisco post-office one morning, in the year 185—, a tall, dark-skinned man placed himself in front of me, and fixing his intensely glittering eyes upon me, said in an excited tone—

"Sir, can you give me a half hour of your time this morning?"

"Yes," I replied, "if I can be of any service to you by so doing."

"Not here, but in your office, privately," he continued. "I must speak to somebody, and having heard you preach in the church on Pine street, I felt that I could approach you. I am in great trouble and danger, and must speak to some one!"

His manner was excited, his hand trembled, and his eye had an insane gleam as he spoke. We walked on in silence until we reached my office on Montgomery street. After entering, I laid down my letters and papers, and was about to offer him a chair, when he hurriedly locked the door on the inside, saying as he did so—

"This conversation is to be private, and I do not intend to be interrupted."

As he turned toward me I saw that he had a pistol in his hand, which he laid on a desk, and then sat down. I waited for him to speak, eyeing him and the pistol closely, and feeling a little uncomfortable, locked in thus with an armed madman of almost giant-like size and strength. The pistol had a sinister look that I had never before recognized in that popular weapon. It seemed to grow bigger and bigger.

"Have you ever been haunted by the idea of suicide?" he asked abruptly, his eyes glaring upon me as he spoke.

"No, not particularly," I answered; "but why do you ask?"

"Because the idea is haunting *me*," he said in an agitated tone, rising from his chair as he spoke. "I have lain for two nights with a cocked pistol in my hand, calculating the value of my life. I bought that pistol to shoot myself with, and I wonder that I have not done it; but something has held me back."

"What has put the idea of suicide into your mind?" I inquired.

"My life's a failure, sir; and there is nothing

else left for such a fool as I have been," he said bitterly. "When a man has no hope left, he should die."

I was making some reply, when he broke in—

"Hear my history, and then tell me if death is not the only thing left for me," laying his hand upon the pistol as he spoke.

When he told me his name I recognized it as that of a man of genius, whose contributions to a certain popular periodical had given him a wide fame in the world of letters. He was the son of a venerable New England Bishop, and a graduate of Harvard University. I will give his story in his own words, as nearly as I can:

"In 1850 I started to California with honorable purpose and high ambition. My father being a clergyman, and poor, and greatly advanced in years, I felt that it was my duty to make provision for him and for the family circle to which I belonged, and of which I was the idol. Animated by this purpose, I was full of hope and energy. On the ship that took me to California I made the acquaintance and fell into the snares of a beautiful but unprincipled woman, for whom I toiled and sacrificed every thing for eight years of weakness and folly, never remitting a dollar to those I had intended to provide for at home, carrying all the while an uneasy conscience and despising myself.

I made immense sums of money, but it all went for nothing but to feed the extravagance and recklessness of my evil genius. Tortured by remorse, I made many struggles to free myself from the evil connection that blighted my life, but in vain. I had almost ceased to struggle against my fate, when Death lifted the shadow from my path. The unhappy woman died, and I was free. I was astonished to find how rapid and how complete was the reaction from my despair. I felt like a new man. The glowing hopes that had been smothered revived, and I felt something of the buoyancy and energy with which I had left my New England hills. I worked hard, and prospered. I made money, and saved it, making occasional remittances to the family at home, who were overjoyed to hear from me after my long and guilty silence. I had n't the heart to write to them while pursuing my evil life.

"I had learned to gamble, of course, but now I resolved to quit it. For two years I kept this resolution, and had in the meantime saved over six thousand dollars. Do you believe that the devil tempts men? I tell you, sir, it is true! I began to feel a strange desire to visit some of my old haunts. This feeling became intense, overmastering. My judgment and conscience protested, but I felt like one under a spell. I yielded, and found my way to a well-known gambling-hell, where I lost every dollar of my hard-earned money. It was like a dream—I seemed to be drawn on to my ruin by some invisible but resistless evil power. When I had lost all, a strange calm came over me, which I have never understood. It may have been the reaction, after nights of feverish excitement, or possibly it was the unnatural calm that follows the death of hope. My self-contempt was complete. No language could have expressed the intensity of my self-scorn. I sneaked to my lodgings, feeling that I had somehow parted with my manhood as well as my money.

"The very next day I was surprised by the offer of a lucrative subordinate position in a federal office in San Francisco. This was not the first coincidence of the sort in my life, where an unexpected influence had been brought to bear upon me, giving my plans and prospects a new direction. Has God any thing to do with these things? or is it accident? I took the place which was offered to me, and went to work with renewed hope and energy. I made a vow against gambling, and determined to recover all I had thrown away. I saved every dollar possible, pinching myself in my living, and supplementing my liberal salary by literary labors. My savings had again run high up in the thousands, and my gains were steady. The Frazer

River mining excitement broke out. An old friend of mine came to me and asked the loan of a hundred dollars to help him off to the new mines. I told him he should have the money, and that I would have it ready for him that afternoon. After he had left, the thought occurred to me that one hundred dollars was a very poor outfit for such an enterprise, and that he ought to have more. Then the thought was suggested—yes, sir, it was *suggested*—that I might take the hundred dollars to a faro-bank and win another hundred to place in the hands of my friend. I was fully resolved to risk not a cent beyond this. The idea took possession of my mind, and when he came for the money I told him my plan, and proposed that he accompany me to the gambling-hell. He was a free-and-easy sort of fellow, and readily assented. We went together, and after alternate successes and losses at the faro-bank, it ended in the usual way: I lost the hundred dollars. I went home in a frenzy of anger and self-reproach. The old passion was roused again. A wild determination to break the faro-bank took hold upon me. I went night after night, betting recklessly until not a dollar was left. This happened last week. Can you wonder that I have concluded there is no hope for as weak a fool as I am?"

He paused a moment in his rapid recital, pacing

the floor with his hand on the hammer of the pistol, which he had taken up.

"Now, sir, candidly, don't you think that the best thing I can do is to blow out my brains?" said he, cocking the pistol as he spoke.

The thought occurred to me that it was no uncommon thing for the suicidal to give way to the homicidal mania. The man was evidently half mad, and ready for a tragedy. That pistol seemed almost instinct with conscious evil intention. If a suicide or a homicide was to end the scene, I preferred the former.

"How old are you?" I asked, aiming to create a diversion.

"I am forty-five," he answered, apparently brought to a little more *recollection* of himself by the question.

"I should think," I continued, having arrested his attention, "that whatever may have been your follies, and however dark the future you have to face, you have too much manhood to sneak out of life by the back-door of suicide."

The shot struck. An instantaneous change passed over his countenance. Suicide appeared to him in a new light—as a cowardly, not an heroic act. He had been fascinated with the notion of having the curtain fall upon his career amid the blaze of blue lights, and the glamour of romance and the dignity of tragedy, amid the wonder of the crowd and the tears of the sentimental. That was all gone—the suicide was but a poor creature, weak as well as wicked. He was saved. He sank into a chair as he handed me the pistol, which I was very glad indeed to get into my hands.

"You should be ashamed of yourself, sir," I continued. "You are only forty-five years old; you are in perfect health, with almost a giant's strength, a classical education, extensive business experience, and with a knowledge of the world gained by your very mistakes that should be a guarantee against the possibility of their repetition. A brave man should never give up the battle—the bravest men never give up."

"Give me the pistol," he said quietly; "you need not be afraid to trust me with it. The devil has left me. I will not act the part of a coward. You will hear from me again. Permit me to thank you. Good-morning."

I did hear from him again. The devil seemed indeed to have left him. He went to British Columbia, where he prospered in business and got rich, became a pillar in the Church of which his father was one of the great lights, and committed not suicide, but matrimony, marrying a sweet and cultured English girl, who thinks her tall Yankee husband the handsomest and noblest of men.

STEWART.

I FIRST met him in New Orleans, in February, 1855. He was small, sandy-haired and whiskered, blue-eyed, bushy-headed, with an impediment in his speech, rapid in movement, and shy in manner. We were on our way to California, and were fellow-missionaries. At the Advocate office, on Magazine street, he was discussed in my presence. "He won't do for California," said one who has since filled a large space in the public eye; "he won't do for that fast country—he is too timid and too slow." Never did a keen observer make a greater mistake in judging a man.

Stewart stood with us on the deck of the *Daniel Webster* that afternoon as we swept down the mighty Mississippi, taking a last, lingering look at the shores we were leaving, perhaps forever, and gazing upon the glories of the sunset on the Gulf. I remember well the feelings of mingled sadness, and curiosity, and youthful hopefulness, that swayed me, until just as the twilight deepened into darkness we struck the long, heavy sea-swell, and I lost at once my sentiment and my dinner. Sea-sickness is the only very distinct remembrance of those days on the Gulf. Sea-sick—sea-sicker—sea-sickest! Stewart succumbed at once. He was very sick, and very low-spirited. One day in the Caribbean Sea, he had crawled out of his hot state-room to seek a breath of fresh air under the awning on deck. He looked unutterably miserable as he said to me—

"Do you believe in presentiments?"

"Yes, I do," was my half-jocular reply.

"So do I," he said with great solemnity; "and I have had a presentiment ever since we left New Orleans that we should never reach California, that we should be caught in a storm, and the ship and all on board lost."

"*I* have had a presentiment," I answered, "that we *shall* arrive safe and sound in San Francisco, and that we *shall* live and labor many years in California, and do some good. Now, I will put my presentiment against yours."

He looked at me sadly, and sighed as he looked out upon the boiling sea that seemed like molten copper under the midday blaze of the tropical sun, and no more was said about presentiments.

He was with us at Greytown, where we went

ashore and got our first taste of tropical scenery, and where we declined a polite invitation from a native to dine on stewed monkey and boiled iguana. (The iguana is a species of big lizard, highly prized as a delicacy by the Nicaraguans.) He enjoyed with us the sights and adventures of the journey across the isthmus. This was a new world to him and us, and not even the horrible profanity and vulgarity of the ninety "roughs" who came in the steerage from New York could destroy the charm and glory of the tropics. Among those ninety drinking, swearing, gambling fellows, there were ninety revolvers, and as we ascended the beautiful San Juan River, flowing between gigantic avenues of lofty teak and other trees, and past the verdant grass-islands that waved with the breeze, and swayed with the motion of the limpid waters, the volleys of oaths and fire-arms were alike incessant. Huge, lazy, rusty-looking alligators lined the banks of the river by hundreds, and furnished targets for these free-and-easy Americans, who had left one part of their country for its good, to seek a field congenial to their tastes and adapted to their talents. The alligators took it all very easy in most cases, rolling leisurely into the water as the bullets rattled harmlessly against their scaly sides. One lucky shot hit a great monster in the eye, and he bounded several feet into the air, and lashed the water into foam with his struggles, as the steamer swept out of sight. The sport was now and then enlivened by the appearance of a few monkeys, at whom (or which) the revolvered Americans would blaze away as they (the monkeys) clambered in fright to the highest branches of the trees. Whisky, profanity, and gunpowder—three things dear to the devil, and that go well together—ruled the day, and gave proof that North American civilization had found its way to those solitudes of nature. Birds of gayest plumage fluttered in the air, and on either hand the forest blazed in all the vividness of the tropical flora. Now and then we would meet a bungo, a long, narrow river-boat, usually propelled by oars worked by eight tawny fellows whose costume was—a panama hat and a cigar! Despite their primitive style of dress; their manners contrasted favorably with the fellow-passengers of whom I have spoken. But I must hurry on, nor suffer this sketch to be diverted from its proper course. How we had to stop at night on the river and lie on the open deck, while the woods echoed with the revelry of the "roughs"—how we were detained at Fort Castilio, and how I fared sumptuously, being taken for a "Padre"—how I didn't throw the contemptible little whiffet who commanded the lake steamer overboard for his unbearable insolence—how we landed in the surf at San Juan del Sur, and got drenched—how we rode mules in the darkness—how nearly we escaped a massacre when a drunken American slapped the face of a native at the "Half-way House," and got stabbed for it, and five hundred muskets and the ninety revolvers were about to be used in shooting —how we averted the catastrophe by a little strategy, and galloped away on our mules, the ladies thundering along after in Concord wagons—how at midnight we reached the blue Pacific, and gave vent to our joy in rousing cheers—and how in due time we passed the Golden Gate in the night, and waked up in San Francisco harbor—may not be told, farther than what is given in this paragraph.

Stewart was sent to the mines to preach. This suited him. Some men shrink from hardships; he seemed to dread only an easy place. Walking his mountain circuit, sleeping in the rude miners' cabins, and sharing their rough fare, he was looked upon as a strange sort of man, who loved toil and forgot self. Such a man he was. His greatest joy was the thought that he could do a work for his Master where others could not or would not go. It was with this feeling that he took the work of agent for the Church-paper and the college, and wandered over California and Oregon doing what was intensely repugnant to his natural feelings. He once told me that he had been such a sinner in his youth that he felt it was right that he should bear the heaviest cross. The idea of penance unconsciously entered into his view of Christian duty, and when he was "roughing it" in the mountains in midwinter, his letters were most cheerful in tone. In the city he was restive, and the more comfortable were his quarters the more eager was he to get away. He had fits of fearful mental depression at times, when he would pass whole nights rapidly pacing his room, with sighs, and groans, and tears. His temper was quick and hot. At a camp-meeting in Sacramento county, he astonished beyond measure a disorderly fellow by giving him a sudden and severe caning. After it was over, Stewart's shame and remorse were great. Everybody else, however, applauded the deed. He had seen service as a soldier in the Mexican war, and was noted for his daring, but now that he belonged to a non-combatant order, he was mortified that for the moment his martial instincts had prevailed. His moral courage was equal to any test. No man dealt more plainly and sternly with the prevalent vices of California, nor dealt more faithfully with a friend. Many a gambler and debauchee winced under his reproofs, and many a Methodist preacher and layman had his eyes opened by his rebukes. But he was tender as well as faithful, and he rarely gave offense. He loved, and was loved by, little children; and there is no stronger proof of a pure and gentle nature than that. He was a Protestant Carmelite, shunning ease, and glorying only in what the flesh naturally abhors. He would have been pained by popularity, in the usual sense of the word. Any unusual attention distressed him, and he always shrank from observation, except when duty called him out. A graduate of Davidson College, North Carolina, and a graduate in medicine, he was more anxious to conceal his learning than most men are to parade theirs. But the luster of such a jewel could not be hid, and that popular instinct which recognizes true souls had given Stewart his proper rank before his fellow-preachers knew his full value. A single product of his brain is in my possession. Bigots and exclusivists in the Churches may miss the meaning. Men are bigots, and do n't know it.

THE PARABLE OF THE FISHERMEN.

A certain great king ordered two companies of fishermen to go out and fish in a large stream that flowed through his dominions, and in the evening bring in the fruits of their day's toil, to supply the tables of the Royal Palace. The companies went out early in the morning, and began to fish. Soon, however, Company A claimed the whole stream, and tried to drive away Company B. Every effort, fair and unfair, was put forth to this end. Whenever, especially, Company B succeeded in taking any fish, then a cruel and relentless war was waged against them; a part of Company A was at once sent to muddy the water, to break their nets, and to make such dreadful noises as to frighten away the fish. Under these disadvantages, if Company B were able to take any fish, a great effort was made to rob their basket, and put them in the basket of Company A. If Company A could not get them out of the basket of Company B, the next effort was to so *damage* them as to render them utterly unfit for use.

Now all this was done when there was plenty of room for both companies, and more fish than both of them could possibly take. Indeed, multitudes of fish were frightened away by the noise, and swam out into shallows, and bogs, and quagmires. Such quantities thus perished that the land stank because of them, and a dreadful pestilence followed. Then the king was wroth. But who was to blame?

When evening was now come, both companies had caught a few little fishes, but a part of these few were seriously damaged. They returned to the palace with misgivings, and presented their almost empty baskets. J. C. S.

Yankee Jims, July 11, 1858.

(Stewart claimed that he belonged to "Company B"—as all do, as does everybody else.)

When the war broke out in 1861, Stewart was preaching in Los Angeles county. The roar of the great struggle reached him, and he became restless. He felt that he ought to share the dangers and sufferings of the South. In reply to a letter from him asking my advice, I advised him not to go. But in a few days I got a note from him, saying that he had prayed over the matter, and felt it his duty to go—he was needed in the hospital work, and he could not shrink. I doubt not there was a subtile attraction to him in the danger and hardship to be met and endured. The next news was that he had started across Mexico to the Rio Grande alone, on horseback, with his saddle-bags, Bible, and hymn-book.

Shortly after crossing the Mexican border, he fell in with a man who gave his name as McManus, who told him he also was bound to Texas, and offered his company. Stewart consented, and they rode on together in what proved to be the path of fate to both. On the third day that they had journeyed in company, they stopped in a lonely place under the shade of some trees near a spring of water to rest and eat. As usual, Stewart read a chapter or two in his pocket-Bible, and then took out his diary and began to write. McManus now saw the opportunity he was seeking. Seizing Stewart's gun, he placed the muzzle against his breast, and fired. He staggered back and fell, the life-blood gushing from his heart, and with a few gasps and moans he was dead. The last words he had just traced in his diary were these: "Lord Jesus, guide and keep me this day." Providence has presented to my mind no greater or sadder mystery than such a death for such a man.

McManus rode back to the little town of Rosario, scarcely caring to conceal his awful crime among the desperadoes with whom he associated. He rode Stewart's horse, and took, with the well-worn saddle-bags, the Bible, the hymn-book, and the eight hundred dollars in gold which had led him to commit the cruel murder. A small party of Texans happened to be passing through that region, who, hearing what had been done, arrested the murderer; but McManus's Mexican friends interfered, and forced the Texans to liberate him. But the devil lured the murderer on to his fate. He started again toward the Rio Grande, still mounted on the murdered preacher's horse, and again he fell into the hands of the Texans. What befel him then was not stated definitely in the narrative given by one of the party. It was merely said, "McManus will kill no more preachers." This does not leave a very wide field for the exercise of the imagination. Stewart was buried where he met his strange and tragic end. Of all the men who bore the banner of the cross in the early days of California, there was no truer or knightlier soul than his.

THE ETHICS OF GRIZZLY HUNTING.

ON the Petaluma boat I met him. He was on his way to Washington City, for the purpose of presenting to the President of the United States a curious chair made entirely of buck-horns, a real marvel of ingenuity, of which he was quite vain. Dressed in buckskin, with fringed leggings and sleeves, belted and bristling with hunters' arms, strongly built and grizzly-bearded, he was a striking figure as he sat the center of a crowd of admirers. His countenance was expressive of a mixture of brutality, cunning, and good humor. He was a thorough animal; wild frontier life had not sublimated this old sinner in the way pictured by writers who romance about such things at a distance. Contact with nature and Indians does not seem to exalt the white man, except in fiction. It tends rather to draw him back toward barbarism. The renegade white only differs from the red savage in being a shade more devilish.

"This is Seth Kinman, the great Indian-fighter and bear-hunter," said an officious passenger.

Thus introduced, I shook hands with him. He seemed inclined to talk, and was kind enough to say he had heard of me, and voted for me. Making due acknowledgment of the honor done me, I seated myself near enough to hear, but not so near as to catch the fumes of the alcoholic stimulants of which he was in the habit of indulging freely. His talk was of himself, in connection with Indians and bears. He seemed to look upon them in the same light—as natural enemies, to be circumvented or destroyed as opportunity permitted.

"You can't trust an Injun," he said; "I know 'em. If they git the upper-hand of you, they'll cinch you, sure. The only way to git along with 'em is to make 'em afeard of you. They'd put a arrer through me long ago if I hadn't made 'em believe I was a *conjurer*. It happened this way: I had a contract for furnishin' venison for the troops in Humboldt, and took along a lot of Injuns for the hunt. We had mighty good luck, and started back to Eureka loaded down with the finest sort of deer-meat. I saw the Injuns laggin' behind, and whisperin' to one another, and mistrusted things wasn't exactly right. So I keeps my eye on 'em, and had old Cottonblossom here [caressing a long, rusty-looking rifle] ready in case any thing should turn up. You can't trust a Injun—they're all alike; if they git the upper-hand of you, you're gone!"

He winked knowingly and chuckled, and then went on:

"I stopped and let the Injuns come up, and then got to talkin' with 'em about huntin' and shootin'. I told 'em I was a conjurer, and couldn't be killed by a bullet or arrer, and to prove it I took off my buckskin shirt and set it up twenty steps off, and told 'em the man who could put a arrer through it might have it. They were more than a hour shootin' at that shirt—the same I've got on now—but they couldn't *faze* it."

"How was that?" asked an open-mouthed young fellow, blazing with cheap jewelry.

"Why, you see, young man, this shirt is well tanned and tough, and I just stood it up on the edges, so that when a arrer struck it, it would naturally give way. If I had only had it on, the arrers would have gone clean through it, and me too. Injuns are mighty smart in some things, but they all believe in devils, conjurin', and such like. I played 'em fine on this idee, and they were afeard to touch me, though they were ready enough if they had dared. While I was out choppin' wood one day, I see a smoke risin', and thinkin' somethin' must be wrong, I got back as soon as I could, and sure enough my house was burnin'. I know'd it was Injuns, and circlin' round I found the track of a big Injun; it was plain enough to see where he had crossed the creek comin' and goin'. I got *his* skelp—why, his har was that long," he said, measuring to his elbow, and leering hideously.

Whether or not this incident was apocryphal I could not decide, but it was evident enough that he intensely relished the notion of "skelping" an Indian.

."I want you to come up to Humboldt and see me kill a grizzly," he continued, addressing himself to me. "An' let me tell you now, if ever you shoot a grizzly, hit him about the ear. If you hit him right, you will kill him; if you do n't kill him, you spile his mind. I have seen a grizzly, after he had been hit about the ear, go round an' round like a top. No danger in a bar after you have hit him in the ear—it 's his tender place. But a bar 's mighty dangerous if you hit him anywhere else, an' do n't kill him. Me an' a Injun was huntin' in a chaparral, and cum across a big grizzly. We both blazed away at him at close range. I saw he was hit, for he whirled half roun', and partly keeled over; but he got up and started for us, mad as fury. We had no time to load, and there was nothin' left but to run for it. It was nip and tuck between us. I 'm a good runner, and the Injun was n't slow.

Lookin' back, I saw the bar was gainin' on us. I know'd he'd git one of us, and so I hauled off and knocked the Injun down. Before he could git up the bar had him."

He paused, and looked around complacently.

"Did the bear kill the Indian?" asked the young man with abundant jewelry.

"No; he *chawed* him up awhile, and then left him, and the Injun finally got well. If it had been a white man, he would have died. Injuns can stand a great deal of hurtin' and not die."

At this point the thought came into my mind that if this incident must be taken as a true presentation of the ethics of bear-hunting as practiced by Mr. Kinman, *I* did not aspire to the honor of becoming his hunting companion. Are the ethics of the stock exchange any higher than those of the Humboldt bear-hunter? Let the bear, bankruptcy, or the devil take the hindmost, is the motto of human nature on its dark side, whether on Wall street or in the California chaparral.

"Was you ever in Napa City?" he inquired of me.

I answered in the affirmative.

"Did you see the big stuffed grizzly in the drugstore? You have, eh? Well, I killed that bar, the biggest ever shot in Californy. I was out one day lookin' for a deer about sundown, and heerd the dogs a-barkin' as they was comin' down Eel River. In a little while here come the bar, an' a whopper he was! I raised old Cottonblossom, and let him have it as he passed me. I saw I had hit him, for he seemed to drag his *lines* [loins] as he plunged down the bank of the river among the grape-vines and thick bushes. Next mornin' I took the dogs and put 'em on his trail. I could see that his back was broke, because I could see the print where his hind-parts had dragged down the sandy bed of the river. By and by I heerd the dogs a-bayin', and I know'd they'd come up with him. I hurried up, and found the bar sittin' on his rump in a hole of water about three feet deep, snappin' his teeth at the dogs as they swum around him, barkin' like fury. He couldn't git any further —old Cottonblossom had done his work for him. I thought I would have a little fun by aggravatin' him awhile."

"What do you mean by aggravating the bear?" asked a bystander.

"I would just take big rocks and go up close to him, and hit him between the eyes. You ought to have heerd him *yowl!* His eyes actually turned green, he was so mad, and his jaws champed like a saw-mill; but he couldn't budge—every time he tried to git on his feet he fell back agin, the maddest bar ever seen."

At this point in the narration Kinman's sinister blue eyes gleamed with brute ferocity. My aversion to making him my hunting companion increased.

"After I had my fun with him, I took old Cottonblossom and planted a bullet under his shoulder, and he tumbled over dead. It took four of us to pull him out of that hole, and he weighed thirteen hundred pounds."

I had enough of this, and left the group, reflecting on the peculiar ethics of bear-hunting. The last glimpse I had of this child of nature, he was chuckling over a grossly obscene picture which he was exhibiting to some congenial spirits. His invitation to join him in a bear-hunt has not yet been accepted.

A MENDOCINO MURDER.

AMONG my occasional hearers when I preached on Weber Avenue, in Stockton, was a handsome, sunny-faced young man who, I was informed, was studying for the ministry of the Presbyterian Church. His manners were easy and graceful, his voice pleasant, his smile winning, and his whole appearance prepossessing to an unusual degree. He was one of the sort of men that everybody likes at first sight. I lost trace of him when I left the place, but retained a decidedly pleasant remembrance of him, and a hopeful interest in his welfare and usefulness. My surprise may be imagined when, a few years afterward, I found him in jail charged with complicity in one of the most horrible murders ever perpetrated in any country.

It was during my pastorate in Santa Rosa, in 187—, that I was told that Geiger, a prisoner confined in the county jail, awaiting trial for murder, had asked to see me. Upon visiting him in his cell, I found that his business with me was not concerning his soul, but his family. They were very poor, and since his imprisonment matters had been going worse and worse with them, until they were in actual want. Knowing well the warm-hearted community of Santa Rosa, I did not hesitate to promise in their name relief for his wife and children. After having satisfied him on this point, I tried to lead the conversation to the subject of religion, but seeing he was not disposed to talk farther, I withdrew. Before leaving the jail, however, I was asked to visit another prisoner charged with participation in the same murder. On going into his cell, the recognition was mutual. It was Alexander, whom I had known, and to whom I had preached at Stockton.

"I little thought when I saw you last that we would meet in such a place as this," he said, with emotion.

"How comes it that you are here? Surely you cannot be the murderer of a woman?" I asked, perhaps a little abruptly.

"It is a curious case, and a long story," he said; "it will all come out on the trial."

I looked at him with an interrogation point in my eyes. Could that pale, meditative, scholarly-looking young man be capable of taking part in such a dark tragedy as that of the murder of which he had been accused? I left him inclined to pronounce him innocent, despite the strong evidence against him. But the conviction of many, who watched the trial a few months after, was clear that he was one of Mrs. Strong's slayers.

Briefly given, here is the story of the murder as gathered from the evidence on the trial, and recollected after the lapse of several years:

Mrs. Strong was a middle-aged woman, with the violent temper and hardened nature so often met with in women who have been subjected to the influences of such a life as she had led—among rough men, and in a rough country where might too often makes right. Geiger and Alexander lived not far from the Strongs, in the wildest region of Mendocino county. A quarrel arose between these two men on one side, and Mrs. Strong on the other, concerning land, the particulars of which have passed my memory. It seems that the right of the case lay rather with the men, and that Mrs. Strong, with a woman's peculiar talent for provocation, rather presumed on her sex in ignoring their claims, at the same time forfeiting all right to consideration on that score by violent language and unwomanly taunts whenever she met them. According to the most charitable theory (and to me it seems the most reasonable), Geiger and Alexander, previously angered by unreasonable opposition, accidentally met Mrs. Strong in a piece of woods. The subject of dispute was brought up, and it is supposed that the unfortunate woman became more and more violent and abusive, until finally, maddened by her words, one of the men, Geiger, it is supposed, struck her down. Then, seeing that she was injured fatally, and fearing discovery, he and Alexander finished the job, and fastening a heavy stone to her neck, hid the body in one of the darkest holes of the stream that flowed through those wild hills, piling stones on the breast and limbs of the corpse to insure concealment.

Of course Mrs. Strong was missed, and search for her began, in which her two murderers were forced to join. What a terrible time that was for the two men—those rides through the woods and cañons, a hundred times passing the dreadful spot, with its awful secret! Surely worse punishment on earth for their terrible crime could not be conceived. Those two instruments of human torture which the Inquisition has never surpassed, Remorse and Fear, were both gnawing at the hearts of these wretched men during all of that long and futile search. But it was given up at last, and they breathed easier.

A few weeks after, an Indian on his pony, riding through the woods, felt thirsty, and turned down the cañon to a spot where the trees stood thick, and the rocks jutted out over the water like greedy monsters looking at their helpless prey beneath. He stooped to quench his thirst in the primitive fashion, but before his lips had touched the water his roving eye caught sight of a swaying something a little way up the stream that made even that stolid red man shrink from drinking that sparkling fluid, for it had flowed over the body of a dead woman. Mrs. Strong was found. The force of the stream had washed away the weighting-stones from the lower limbs, and the stream having fallen several feet since the heavy rains of the past weeks, the feet of the corpse were visible above the water. The stone was still attached to the neck, thus keeping all but those ghastly feet under the water. The long-hidden murder was out at last, and the quiet Indian riding away on his tired pony carried with him the fate of Geiger and Alexander. When the news was told, it was remembered how unwilling they had been to search near that spot, and how uneasy and excited they had seemed whenever it was approached. Indeed, they had been objects of suspicion to many, and the discovery of the body was followed immediately by their arrest. The trial resulted in the acquittal of Alexander, the justice of which was questioned by many, and a sentence of life-long imprisonment for Geiger. Before his removal to the State-prison, however, he made his escape, aided, it is supposed, by his wife, who is thought to have brought him tools for that purpose secreted in her clothing. He has never been found, and in all probability never will be. Some say he has never left the county, and is living the life of a wild animal in the mountains there; but it is more likely that he, like the first murderer, fled to far lands, where he must ever bear the scarlet letter of Remorse in his heart.

BEN.

BEN was a black man. His African blood was unmixed. His black skin was true ebony, his lips were as thick as the thickest, his nose was as flat as the flattest, his head as woolly as the woolliest. His immense lips were red, and their redness was not a mark of beauty, only giving a grotesque effect to a physiognomy no part of which presented the least element of the æsthetic. He had neither feet nor legs, but was quite a lively pedestrian, shuffling his way on his stumps, which were protected by thick leather coverings.

Ben, when I first knew him, kept a boot-black stand near the post-office in San Francisco. He also kept postage-stamps on sale. He was talkative, and all his talk was about religion. His patrons listened with wonder or amusement. A boot-black that talked religion in the very vortex of the seething sea of San Francisco mammonism, was a new thing. And then Ben's quaint way of speaking lent a special interest to his words, and his enjoyment of his one theme was catching. He was more given to the relation of experience than to polemics. When he touched upon some point that moved him, he would unconsciously pause in his work, his exulting voice arresting the attention of many a hurried passer-by, as he spoke of the love of Jesus, and of the peace of God.

He slept at night in the little cage of a place in which he polished boots and shoes by day. Many a time when I have passed the spot at early dawn, on my way to take the first boat for Sacramento, I have heard his voice singing a hymn inside. A lark's matin song could not be freer or more joyful. It seemed to be the literal bubbling over of a soul full of love and joy. The melody of Ben's morning song has followed me many and many a mile, by steam-boat and by rail. It was the melody of a soul that had learned the sublime secret which the millionaires of the metropolis might well give their millions to buy.

Ben had been a slave in Missouri in the old days *ante bellum*. He spoke kindly of his former owners, who had treated him well. Being liberated, he emigrated to California, and found his way to San Francisco—a waif that had floated into a new world.

"How came you to be so crippled, Ben?" I asked him one day as he was lingering on the final touches on my second boot, being in one of his happiest and most voluble moods.

"My feet and legs got froze in Mizzoory, sir, and dey had to be cut off."

"That was a hard trial for you, wasn't it?"

"No, sir, it didn't hurt me as much as I 'spected it would, an' I know'd it was all for de bes', else 't wouldn't have happened ter me. De loss o' dem legs don't keep me from gittin' about, an' my health's as good as anybody's. De Lord treats me kin', and mos' everybody has a kind word for Ben. Bless God, he makes me happy widout legs!"

The plantation *patois* clave to Ben, and among the sounds of the many-tongued multitude of San Francisco, it had a charm to ears to which it was familiar in early days. It was like the song of a land-bird at sea.

Ben had a great joy when his people bought and moved into their house of worship. He gave a hundred dollars, which he had laid by for that object a dime at a time. It made him happier to give that money than to have been remembered in Vanderbilt's will.

"I wanted ter give a hundred dollars to help buy de house, an' I know de Lord wanted me to do it, too, 'cause de customers poured in an' kep' me busy all day long. Once in awhile a gentleman would han' me a quarter, or half a dollar, an' would n't wait for change. I know'd what dat meant—it was for dat hundred dollars."

Ben's big, dull, white eyes were not capable of much expression, but his broad, black face beamed with grateful satisfaction as he gave me this little bit of personal history. A trustee of his Church told me that they were not willing at first to take the money from Ben, but that they saw plainly it would not do to refuse. It was the fulfillment of a cherished object that he had carried so long in his simple, trusting heart, that to have rejected his gift would have been cruelty.

The last time I saw Ben he was working his way along a crowded thoroughfare, dragging his heavy leathers, his head reaching to the waist of the average man.

"How are you, Ben?" I said, as we met.

"Bless God, I'm first-rate!" he said, grasping my hand warmly, his face brightening, and every tooth visible. It was clear he had not lost the secret.

Ben was not a Methodist—he was what is popularly called a Campbellite.

OLD TUOLUMNE.

THE former residents of Tuolumne county, California, meet once a year in some city or town, and celebrate "auld lang-syne" by an oration, a poem, a dinner, and other exercises. These occasions become more interesting as the old times recede. The author of this little volume was called to the office of poet laureate in 1875, and these verses are the result:

    The bearded men in rude attire,
    With nerves of steel, and hearts of fire—
    The women few, but fair and sweet,
    Like shadowy visions dim and fleet—

    Again I see, again I hear,
    As through the past I dimly peer,
    And muse o'er buried joy and pain,
    And tread the hills of youth again.

    As speeds the torrent, strong and wild,
    Adown the mountains roughly piled,
    To find the plain, and there to sink
    In thirsty sands that eager drink

Old Tuolumne.

The streams that toward the ocean flow,
As on, and ever on, they go—
Their course as brief, their doom as sure—
A rush, a flash, and all is o'er!—

So tides of life that early rolled
Through old Tuolumne's hills of gold,
Are spread and lost in other lands,
Or swallowed in the desert sands,

Where manhood's strength and beauty's bloom
Have rushed to meet the common doom;
The arm of might, the heart of love,
The soul that soared to worlds above;

The high intent that scaled the heights
Where false Ambition's treacherous lights
Delusive shine to mock and cheat
The wretch who climbs with bleeding feet.

O days of youth! O days of power!
Again ye come for one glad hour,
To let us taste once more the joy
That Time may dim, but not destroy.

Again we feel our pulses thrill
To hear sweet voices long since still;
Again Hope's air-built castles bright
Rise up before the enchanted sight.

Ye are not lost! The arm of might,
The smile of beauty and brow of light,
The love, the hope, the high emprise,
The visions born in paradise.

As all the streams that sink from sight
In desert sands, and leave the light,

To the blue seas make silent way,
To swell their tides some future day—

So lives that sink and fade from view,
Like scattered drops of rain or dew,
Shall gather with all deathless souls,
Where the eternal ocean rolls!

CALIFORNIA, June 17, 1875.

THE BLUE LAKES.

IT is not strange that the Indians think the Blue Lakes are haunted, and that even the white man's superstition is not proof against the weird and solemn influence that broods over this spot of almost unearthly beauty. They are about ten miles from Lakeport, the beautiful county-seat of Lake county, which nestles among the oaks on the margin of Clear Lake, a body of water about thirty miles long, and eight miles wide, surrounded by scenery so lovely as to make the visitor forget for the time that there is any ugliness in the world. The first sight of Clear Lake, from the highest point of the great range of hills shutting it in on the south, will never be forgotten by any one who has a soul. After winding slowly up, up, up the mountain road, a sharp turn is made, and you are on the summit. The driver stops his panting team, you spring out of the "thorough-brace," and look, and look, and look. Immediately below you is a sea of hills, stretching away to where they break against the lofty rampart of the coast-range on your left, and in front sinking gradually down into the valley below. The lake lies beneath you, flashing like a mirror in the sunlight, its northern shore marked by rugged brown acclivities, the nearer side dotted with towns, villages, and farms, while "Uncle Sam," the monarch peak of all the region, lifts his awful head into the clouds, the sparkling waters kissing his feet. I once saw "Uncle Sam" transfigured. It was a day of storm. The wind howled among the gorges of the hills, and the dark clouds swept above them in mighty masses, the rain falling in fitful and violent showers. Pausing at the summit to rest the horse, and to get a glance at the scene in its wintry aspect, I drew my gray shawl closer, and leaned forward and gazed. It was about the middle of the afternoon. Suddenly a rift in the clouds westward let the sunshine through, and falling on "Uncle Sam," lo, a miracle! The whole mountain, from base to summit, softened, blushed, and blazed with the prismatic colors. It was a transfiguration. The scene is symbolic. Behind me and about me are cloud and tempest, typing the humanity of the past and the present with its conflicts, and trials, and dangers; before me the glorified mountain, typing the humanity of the future, enveloped in the rainbow of peace, showing that the storms are all over. This was my interpretation to my friend who sat by my side, but I do not insist upon it as canonical.

The Blue Lakes lie among the hills above Clear Lake, and the road leads through dense forests, of which the gigantic white-oaks are the most striking feature. It passes through Scott's Valley, a little body of rich land, the terraced hills behind, and the lake before. Winding upward, the ascent is so gradual that you do not realize, until you are told, that the Blue Lakes are six hundred feet above the level of Clear Lake. The lakes are three in number, and in very high water they are connected. They are each perhaps a mile in length, and only a few hundred yards in width. Their depth is immense. Their waters are a particularly bright blue color, and so clear that objects are plainly seen many fathoms below the surface. They are hemmed in by the mountains, the road being cut in the side of the overhanging bluff, while on the opposite side bold, rugged brown cliffs rise in almost perpendicular walls from the water's edge. A growth of oaks shades the narrow vale between the lakes, and the mountain-pine, and oak, madrona, and manzanita clothe the heights.

There are the Blue Lakes. A solemnity and awe steal over you. Speech seems almost profane. The very birds seem to hush their singing as they flit in silence among the trees. The chatter of a gray squirrel has an audacious sound as the bushy-tailed little hoodlum dashes across the grade, and rushes up a tree. The coo of a turtle-dove away off in a distant cañon falls on the ear like the echo of a human sorrow that had found soothing, but not healing. The sky overhead is as blue as the drapery of Guido's Madonna, and there is just a hint of a breeze sighing over the still waters, like the respiration of a peaceful sleeper. The cliffs above the lake duplicate themselves in the water beneath with startling life-likeness, and with the spell of the place upon you it would scarcely surprise you to see unearthly shapes emerge from the crystal depths, glittering in celestial beauty.

The feeling of superstitious awe is perhaps increased by the knowledge of the fact that no Indian will go near these lakes. They say a monster inhabits the upper lake, and has subterranean communication with the two lower ones, and of this monster they have a mortal terror. This terror is explained by the following legend:

Many, many moons ago, when the Ukiah Indians were a great and strong people, a fair-haired white man, of great stature, came from the sea-shore alone, and took up his abode with them. He knew many things, and was stronger than any warrior of the tribe. The chief took him to his own campoody, and giving him his daughter for his wife, made him his son. She loved the white man, and never tired in looking upon his fair face, and into his bright blue eyes. But by and by the white man, tiring of his Indian bride, and longing to see his own people, turned his face again toward the sea, and fled. She followed him swiftly, and overtaking him at the Blue Lakes, gently reproached him for his desertion of her, and entreated him to return. They were standing on the rock overhanging the lake on its northern side. He took her hand smiling, and spoke deceitful words, and then suddenly seizing her, hurled her with all his strength headlong into the lake. She sank to the bottom, while the white man resumed his flight, and was seen no more. His murdered bride was transformed into an evil genius of the lake. The long and sinuous outline of a serpentine form would be seen on the surface of the water, out of which would be lifted at intervals the head of a woman, with long, bright hair, and sad, filmy, blue eyes, into which whosoever looked would die before another twelve moons had passed.

The Indians would go miles out of their way to avoid the haunted spot, and more than one white man affirmed that they had seen the Monster of Clear Lake.

One stormy day in the winter of eighteen hundred and sixty-something, I was with a friend on my way from Ukiah to Lakeport, by way of the Blue Lakes. After swimming Russian River, always a bold and rapid stream, but then swollen and angry from recent heavy rains, urging our trusty span of horses through the storm, at length we reached the grade winding along above the lakes. The darkened heavens hung pall-like over the waters, the clouds weeping, and the wind moaning. Dense clouds boiled up along the mountain-peaks, veiling their heads in white folds. No sign of life was visible. We drove slowly, and were silent, feeling the spell of the place.

"There's the Monster!" I suddenly exclaimed.

"Where?" asked my companion, starting, and straining his gaze upon the lake below.

There it was—a long, dark mass, with serpent-like movement, winding its way across the lake. It suddenly vanished, without lifting above the water the woman's head with the bright hair and filmy eyes. My companion expressed the prosaic idea that it was a school of fish swimming near the surface, but I am sure we saw all there was of the Monster of the Blue Lakes.

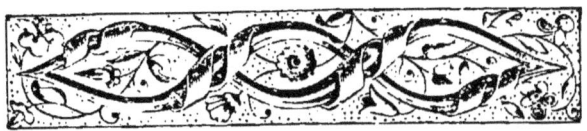

A CALIFORNIA MOUNTAIN ROAD.

WE wound along the mountain way,
   My friend and I, and spake no word;
   We felt that air should but be stirred
By bird's rich note, or wind's soft play.

The deep blue sky to us said, "Hush;"
   The pure, soft air could not bear speech;
   And steep decline, and lofty reach,
Kept silence all with tree and bush.

What need for words when every sense
   Was full to brim? We had no thought,
   But only felt the glow, and caught
The mightiness, the joy intense.

Uplifted high above it all,
   The shrouded maid, St. Helen,* lay;
   From either side there swept away
A stretch of bare, brown earth, the pall.

---

* Mount St. Helena is so called on account of its resemblance to the form of a recumbent maiden, when seen from the south.

A California Mountain Road.

The nearer slopes were clothed in green,
With here and there the topaz flame
Of poison-oak, of deadly fame;
While far below was faintly seen,

In depths of shade, the foaming flow
Of water from the mountain height.
The cañon's sides were hung with light,
Young trees, and starred with flowers' glow.

And oft from out the wild brush-wood,
Like to some slender Indian maid,
Upstarting from the thicket's shade,
The redskin tree, Madrona, stood.

Behind us lay the giant stair,
By which we pigmies reached this height;
Each lessening step in that soft light
Was violet-robed by the magic air.

Ah! that fair day! 'T was crowned, complete;
For that true friend who shared my ride,
And Nature's self who stood beside,
My dearest were, and they did meet.

Since then, my friend has left my side
For Mother Earth's, and buried deep
Where sea-winds wail, he sound doth sleep;
And half is gone from tree and tide.

Though all unchanged that scene may be,
Its charm for me would now be pain.
I could not ride that road again,
My friend in earth, and not with me.

DR. ELEAZAR THOMAS.

"YOU and I are new-comers to California, and having had no part in the strifes in which some of our brethren have been engaged, we will act as peace-makers, and keep these belligerents quiet."

This was the half-playful remark of Dr. Eleazar Thomas, one of a group of preachers sitting in the parlor of the then editor of the *California Christian Advocate*, the Rev. S. D. Simonds, in the spring of 1855. We had taken tea together, and were engaged in free-and-easy conversation in the editor's cottage, high up on Clay Street Hill.

The speaker, like myself, had just arrived in California, in the capacity of a Methodist preacher —he from the North, and I from the South. He was a man of pleasing and commanding presence, tall, ruddy-complexioned, with blue eyes, and lightish hair, with deliberate and distinct enunciation, and a winning manner. Take the best points of a

Presbyterian preacher of the best class, and the best points of a Methodist preacher of the best class, and the combined result would be just such a man as he appeared to me that evening. And now, after the lapse of twenty-four years, this description seems to suit him still. Subsequent events recalled to my mind the remark I have quoted, but with widely different feelings at different times. He became the editor of the Northern Methodist, and I of the Southern Methodist organ, in San Francisco. The *California Christian Advocate* and the *Pacific Methodist* were like batteries planted on Mount Ebal and Mount Gerizim respectively, waking the echoes by their cannonading in many an editorial duel. The war drove us farther and still farther apart in opinion, but every time we met we drew closer to each other in personal attachment. In those unhappy days, many a friendship was hopelessly wrecked by differences of political opinion—a fact which shows how ardent were the convictions on both sides, and explains the fact of a five years' deadly conflict between men speaking the same language, reading the same Bible, praying to the same God, reared under the same constitution, and cherishing the same historic memories. Both sides were in earnest, and it was their sad fate to be compelled to fight out a quarrel bequeathed to them by their glorious but fallible ancestors. The seeds of the civil war of 1861 were sown in the very compromises of the constitution of 1783. At the white heat of the struggle my brother editor wrote things that amazed and angered me. Perhaps if he were speaking now, he would say the same of me. But his mind was naturally conservative and philosophic, and long before the fall of the curtain at Appomattox he had reacted, recovering the tone of moderation and magnanimity of spirit that were natural to him. One day, just after the close of the war, we met on a street-corner. He expressed great satisfaction that the effusion of blood had ceased, paid a glowing tribute to the courage of the vanquished party and the greatness of Lee, and then added, thoughtfully—

"But you may see which side God was on by the result."

"That will not do," I answered; "if the triumph of brute force is to be taken as evidence of the Divine approval, you will have to unread the larger part of history. On that principle, those that crucified Jesus were right, and he was wrong; the mob was right, and Stephen was wrong; Rome was right, and the victims she ground under her iron heel were wrong; Austria was right, and Hungary was wrong; Russia was right, and poor Poland was wrong. As I read history, it teaches that the right has usually been advanced, not by its triumphs on the bloody field, but by the sublime fortitude of its adherents under defeat, and in the midst of suffering and sorrow. If I were to presume to interpret the providence of God, and to infer what are his designs, a different conclusion might be reached. A strong nation conquers the weak nation. The able-bodied ruffian flogs the feeble-bodied saint. Three men in the wrong will, in an appeal to brute force, be more than a match for one in the right. That is the usual course of events. Now and then God makes bare his arm in such a way as to show that the race is not always to the swift, nor the battle to the strong. God may have been on the winning side in the late war, as you say, but it will not do for a Christian man to assume that He is always on the side that prevails on the bloody field. That would be making him *particeps criminis* with every tyrant that has scourged the earth."

"Well, we can at least agree in the hope and prayer that He will overrule all for the good of all in our land, and that with peace may come mutual forgiveness and universal prosperity."

"Yes; I can unite heartily with you in that hope and prayer."

"Give me your hand," he said impulsively; "henceforward we must all stand together, and make the best of the new conditions which have arisen."

He stood to that pledge, meaning what he said. We met frequently, and I always felt that my spirit was sweetened, and my horizon broadened, by intercourse with this strong thinker who had cast aside the strait-jacket of provincialism and bigotry, and whose own vision had a widening range. Agreeing in spirit, our very differences of opinion enhanced the charm of his society and the relish of his conversation. This man was the type of an immense class, both North and South, whose traditions and natural affiliations made them stubborn antagonists in war times, but to whose broad patriotism, conscientious conservatism, and sweet Christian spirit, our country must look for the speedy restoration and perpetual enjoyment of the blessings and benefits of national union. When, as a fraternal delegate to the Pacific Conference (with Dr. M. C. Briggs as associate), held at Vacaville in 1868, after his beautiful and touching address, I rose and extended him my hand in token of fraternity, I did so all the more cordially because I knew that behind his glowing, fraternal words, there was beating a warm, fraternal heart. The scene was dramatic, but not intentionally so, when, as the interview proceeded, the tide of good-feeling rose higher and higher, until, sweeping away all obstructions, fraternity triumphed amid a storm of Amens and a shower of tears. Ecclesiastical prejudice and punctilio could not withstand the swelling current of love which bore that body of Methodist preachers on its bosom. Bishop Marvin was in the chair. They know each other better now, as they stand in the light of God.

When Dr. Thomas was appointed by the President of the United States a peace commissioner to the Modoc Indians, all Californians recognized his fitness for the position. If a peace policy was to be followed, it was proper that a minister of the Prince of Peace should be called into service. Whether the "Quaker policy," so called, was the right one, is a question concerning which the men on the border and the theorists in older communities have always differed. William Penn was successful in dealing with Indians. So were Andrew Jackson, Jack Hays, and General Crook—but in a different way. The history of the Modoc war may be taken as typical of the whole history of our dealings with the Indians. The whites were arbitrary, and the Indians savage and treacherous. The immediate cause of the war was the attempted forcible removal of the Indians to a reservation, in the fall of 1872. The Modocs, who had already a bad reputation, resisted. The small detachment of soldiers sent to remove them was attacked, and, after a brisk fight, the Modocs fled to the hills along the Oregon line, killing twelve or fourteen unfortunate whites on their retreat. The United States soldiers sent to operate against them failed to accomplish any thing farther than to get several of their number killed and scalped. The Indians took refuge in the lava-beds—a mass of volcanic rock in Siskiyou county, California, about three miles wide and six miles long, and in places rising to a considerable height. These rocks are honey-combed with holes and caves, affording shelter and concealment for thousands of men. They are four hundred and eighty miles north of San Francisco, and about two hundred miles from Crescent City, on the extreme northern coast-line of California. Mount Shasta, 14,440 feet above the sea, glacier-crowned, is seventy miles south. Captain Jack, chief of the Modocs, intrenched in this stronghold of nature, defied the United States army, repelling every assault, shooting down the soldiers with impunity. The Indians became more exacting in their demands, believing themselves impregnable. At this juncture the four Peace Commissioners—General Canby, Dr. Thomas, and Dyar and Meacham—met a delegation of Modoc warriors by invitation of Captain Jack, who stipulated that none but the commissioners should be present, and that all should go unarmed. On the morning of May 11,

1873, Captain Jack, with four warriors, issued from the lava-beds, and in a chosen spot met the commissioners. The formalities usual on such occasions were gone through with, several "talks" were had, and the negotiations seemed to be making good progress, when, quick as thought, the treacherous Modoc chief snatched a pistol which he had concealed on his person, and shouting to his men, "*Hetuck!*" "*Hetuck!*" (All ready!) sent a bullet through the head of the brave Canby, who fell dead. Two of the Indians attacked Dr. Thomas, shooting and killing him on the spot where he stood. Meacham was wounded. Dyar escaped unhurt, and fled to camp with the dreadful news.

So ended the mission of the peace-maker, and so died my friend. His body was brought to San Francisco, and was given such a burial as is bestowed only upon heroes and public benefactors. The civil dignitaries of the State and city, the officers and soldiers of the army, the venerable and honored ministers of Christ, and a vast multitude of sorrowful men and women, gathered at the sanctuary on Powell street, where his voice was first heard in San Francisco, uniting to honor a man who lived nobly and died gloriously at the post of duty. To our poor human sight, it seems as if in the battle that is being fought for all that is dear and distinctive in our Christian civilization in California, his wisdom and his valor are needed. Above all, it would seem that his influence is needed to draw good men nearer together for the struggle in which they are all equally interested. But Infinite Wisdom instead gave him the completed beatitude, and left to us the example of the Peace-maker.

FATHER ACOLTI.

I FIRST met him one day in 1857, in the Santa Cruz Mountains. Stopping at a sort of wayside inn near the summit to water my horse, a distinguished-looking man, who stood by his buggy with a bucket in his hand, saluted me—

"Good-morning, sir. You wish to water your horse—may I wait on you?"

His manner would have melted in a moment a whole mountain of conventional ice, it was so cordial and so spontaneous. Disregarding my mild protest against being waited on by my senior, he filled the bucket from the sparkling fountain, and gave it to the thirsty animal, still panting from the long climb up the mountain-side. In the meantime we had exchanged names and occupations—he, Father Acolti, a priest, and teacher in the Jesuit College at Santa Clara; and I, the writer of these humble Sketches. As he stood there before me, he looked like anything rather than a disciple of Ignatius Loyola. He was sturdy and fat, yet refined and graceful in appearance. His features were large, his head massive, his expression one of great benignity, illuminated with frequent flashes of good humor. There was also about him a something that suggested that he had suffered. I fell in love with Father Acolti on the spot. When he drove down the mountain on the one side, and I on the other, it really seemed as if the grand redwoods had caught a friendlier look, and the wild honeysuckles a richer fragrance from the sunny-faced old priest. The tone of human companionship wonderfully modifies the aspects of external nature.

Father Acolti and I met often after this. On the highway, in the social circles of the lovely Santa Clara Valley, and especially in the abodes of sickness and poverty, I crossed his path. He seemed to have an instinct that guided him to the needy and the sorrowing. It is certain that the instinct of suffering souls led them to the presence of the old priest, whose face was so fatherly, whose voice was so gentle, whose eye melted so readily with pity, and whose hand was so quick to extend relief.

There was a tinge of romance in Father Acolti's history. He was an Italian of noble birth. A beautiful woman had given him her heart and hand, and before one year of wedded happiness had passed she died. The young nobleman's earthly hope and ambition died with her. He sold his estates, visited her tomb for the last time, and then, renouncing the world, applied for admission into the mysterious order of the Society of Jesus, an organization whose history makes the most curious chapter in the record of modern religious conflict. Having served his novitiate, he was ready for work. His scientific attainments and tastes naturally drew him to the work of education, and doubtless he heartily responded to the command to repair to California as one of a corps of teachers who were to lay the foundations of an educational system for the Roman Catholic Church. But in reality, the Jesuits had entered California nearly ninety years before, and laid the foundations upon which their successors are now building. The old mission-churches, with their vineyards and orchards, are the monuments of their zeal and devotion. The California Digger Indians were the subjects of the missionary zeal of the early Jesuit Fathers, and whether the defect was in the methods of the teachers, or in the capabilities of their Indian neophytes, the effort to elevate those poor red brethren of ours to the plane of Christian civilization failed. They are still savages, and on the path to extinction. The Digger will become neither a citizen nor a Christian. He is one of the very lowest of the

Father Acolti.

human family, and his room will soon be accepted in place of his company. In the conflict of vigorous races on the Pacific coast, he has no chance to survive. The Jesuits deserve credit for what they attempted in behalf of the Indians. We Protestants, who claim a purer faith, and better methods, have as yet done but little to arrest the process of their extirpation, or elevate them in the scale of humanity. I fear we have been but too ready to conclude that these poor wretches are not included in the command to preach the gospel to every creature. The sight of a Digger Indian camp makes a heavy draft upon Christian faith. But did not the Christ die for them?

One fact in Father Acolti's history invested him with peculiar interest in the minds of the people: He was of noble blood. I do not know how many persons in the Santa Clara Valley whispered this secret to me as a fact of great importance. Democrats and republicans as they are in theory, no people on earth have in their secret hearts a profounder reverence for titles of nobility than the Americans. From Father Acolti himself no hint of any thing of the kind was ever heard. He never talked of himself. Nor did I ever hear him mention his religious views, except in very general terms. It is said, and perhaps truly, that the Jesuits are all propagandists by profession; but this old priest made you forget that he was any thing but a genial and lovable old gentleman with fine manners and a magnetic presence.

After my removal to San Francisco, he too was transferred to the metropolis, and assigned to duty in connection with the Jesuit church and college, on Market street. Here again I found his tracks wherever I went among the poor and the miserable. Whether it was a dying foreigner in the sandhills, a young man without money hunting for work, a poor widow bewildered and helpless in her grief, a woman with a drunken husband and a house full of hungry children, a prisoner in the jail, or a sick man in the hospital, Father Acolti's hand was sure to be found in any scheme of relief. Meeting him on the street, you would catch a glow from his kind face and friendly voice, and in most instances leave him with a smile at some little pleasantry that rippled forth as he stood with his hand resting familiarly on your shoulder. He loved his little joke, but it was never at the expense of any human being, and his merriment never went farther than a smile that brightened all over his broad face. There was that about him that repelled the idea of boisterous mirth. The shadow of a great sorrow still lay in the background of his consciousness, shading and softening his sky, but not obscuring its light. As his step grew feebler, and it became evident that his strength was failing, this shadow seemed to deepen. There was a wistful look in his eyes that spoke of a longing for Italy, for his buried love, or for heaven. There were tears in his eyes when we parted in the street for the last time, as he silently pressed my hand and walked slowly away. I was not surprised when the news reached me soon after that he was dead. And the reader will not be surprised that in penciling these Sketches the image of this sunny-faced old man has looked up to me from the unwritten sheet so often that he appears here in strange company. If I should ever meet him again, I trust it will be where no shadow shall dim the light that will shine on us both.

MY FIRST CALIFORNIA CAMP-MEETING.

A CALIFORNIA camp-meeting I had never seen, and so when the eccentric Dr. Cannon, who was dentist, evangelist, and many other things all at once, sent me an invitation to be present at one that was soon to come off near Vallecito, in Calaveras county, I promptly signified my acceptance, and began preparation for the trip. It was in 1856, when we occupied the parsonage in Sonora that had been bequeathed to us in all its peculiar glory by our bachelor predecessors. It had one room, which served all the purposes of parlor, library, dining-room, and *boudoir*. The book-case was two dry-goods boxes placed lengthwise, one above the other. The safe, or cupboard, was a single dry-goods box, nailed to the red-wood boards, of which the house was built, with cleats for our breakfast, dinner, and tea-sets, which, though mentioned here in the plural form, were singular in more than one sense of the word. The establishment boasted a kitchen, the roof of which was less than the regulation height of the American soldier, the floor of which was made by nature, the one window of which had neither sash nor glass, the door of which had no lock, but was kept shut by a small leather strap and an eight-penny nail and its successors. The thieves did not steal from us— they couldn't. Dear old cabin on the hill-side! It brings up only pleasant memories of a time when life was young, and hope was bright. When we closed the door of the parsonage, and, sitting behind McCarthy & Cooper's two-horse team—one a beautiful white, the other a shining bay—dashed out of town in the direction of the bold and brawling Stanislaus, no fear was felt for any valuables left behind. The prancing of that spirited white horse on the narrow grade that wound its way a thousand feet above the bed of the river was a more serious matter, suggesting the possibility of an adventure that would have prevented the writing of these Sketches. The Stanislaus, having its sources among the springs and snows of the Sierras, was a clear and sparkling stream before the miners muddied it by their digging its banks and its bed for gold. It cuts its way through a wild and rugged region, dashing, foaming, fighting for its passage along narrow passes where the beetling cliffs and toppling crags repel the invasion of a human foot. It seems in hot haste to reach the valley, and fairly leaps down its rocky channel. In high water it roars and rushes with terrific violence. But it was behaving quietly as we passed it, keeping within its narrow channel, along which a number of patient Chinamen were working over some abandoned gold diggings, wearing satisfied looks, indicating success. Success is the rule with the Chinaman. He is acquisitive by nature, and thrifty from necessity. He has taught the conceited Americans some astonishing lessons in the matter of cheap living. But they are not thankful for the instruction, nor are they disposed to reduce it to practice. They are not yet prepared to adopt Asiatic ideas of living and labor. The contact of the two civilizations produces only friction now. What the future may bring forth I will not here prophesy, as this has properly nothing to do with the camp-meeting.

An expected circus had rather thrown the camp-meeting into the background. The highly-colored sensational posters were seen in every conspicuous place, and the talk of the hotel-keepers, hostlers, and straggling pedestrians, was all about the circus. The camp-meeting was a bold experiment, under the circumstances. The camp-ground was less than a mile from Vallecito, a mining camp, whose reputation was such as to suggest the need of special evangelical influences. It was attacking the enemy in his stronghold. The spot selected for the encampment was a beautiful one. On a gentle slope, in the midst of a grove of live-oaks, a few rude tents were pitched, with sides of undressed red-wood, and covered with nothing, so that the stars could be gazed at during the still hours of the cloudless California summer night. The "preacher's stand" was erected under one of the largest of the oaks, in front of which were ranged rough, backless seats, for the accommodation of the worshipers. A well of pure water was close at hand, and a long table, composed of undressed boards, was spread under clustering pines conveniently situated. Nobody thought of a table-cloth, and the crockery used was small in quantity and plain in quality.

During the first day and night of the meeting, small but well-behaved audiences waited upon the word, manifesting apparently more curiosity than religious interest. The second night was a solemn and trying time. The crowd had rushed to the circus. Three or four preachers and about a dozen hearers held the camp-ground. The lanterns, swung in the oaks, gave a dim, uncertain light, the gusts of wind that rose, and fell, and moaned among the branches of the trees threatening their extinguishment every moment. One or two of the lights flickered out entirely, increasing the gloom and the weirdness of the scene. It was a solemn time; the sermon was solemn, the hearers were solemn, and there was a solemnity of cadence in the night-wind. Everybody seemed gloomy and discouraged but the irrepressible Cannon. He was in high glee.

"The Lord is going to do a great work here," he said at the close of the service, rubbing his hands together excitedly.

"What makes you think so?"

"The devil is busy working against us, and when the devil works the Lord is sure to work too. The people are all at the circus to-night, but their consciences will be uneasy. The Holy Spirit will be at work with them. To-morrow night you will see a great crowd here, and souls will be converted."

Perhaps there were few that indorsed his logic, or shared his faith, but the result singularly verified his prophecy. The circus left the camp. The reaction seemed to be complete. A great crowd came out next night, the lights burned more brightly, the faithful felt better, the preachers took fire, penitents were invited and came forward for prayers, and for the first time the old camp-meeting choruses echoed among the Calaveras hills. The meeting continued day and night, the crowd increasing at every service until Sunday. Many a wandering believer, coming in from the hills and gulches, had his conscience quickened and his religious hopes rekindled, and the little handful that sung and prayed at the beginning of the meeting swelled to quite an army.

On Sunday, Bishop Kavanaugh preached to an immense crowd. That eloquent Kentuckian was in one of his inspired moods, and swept every thing before him. For nearly two hours he held the vast concourse of people spell-bound, and toward the end of his sermon his form seemed to dilate, his face kindled into a sort of radiance, and his voice was like a golden trumpet. Amens and shouts burst forth all around the stand, and tears rained from hundreds of eyes long unused to the melting mood. California had her camp-meeting christening that day. Attracted by curiosity, a Digger Indian chief, with a number of "bucks" and squaws, had come upon the ground. The chief had seated himself against a tree on the outer edge of the crowd, and never took his eyes from the Bishop for a moment. I watched him almost as closely as he watched the Bishop, for I was curious to know what were the thoughts passing through his benighted mind, and to see what effect the service would have upon him. His interest seemed to increase as the discourse proceeded. At length he showed signs of profound emotion; his bosom heaved, tears streamed down his tawny cheeks, and finally, in a burst of irrepressible admiration, he pointed to the Bishop, and exclaimed, "*Capitan!*" "*Capitan!*" The chief did not understand English. What was it that so stirred his soul? Was it the voice, the gesture, the play of feature, the magnetism of the true orator? The good Bishop said it was the Holy Spirit—the wind that bloweth where it listeth. The Sunday-night service drew another large audience, and culminated in a great victory. The singing and prayers were kept up away beyond midnight. The impression of one song I shall never forget. The Bishop was my bed-fellow. We had retired for the night, and were stretched on our primitive couch, gazing unobstructed upon the heavenly hosts shining on high.

"Hark! listen to that song," said the Bishop, as a chorus, in a clear, bugle-like voice, floated out upon the midnight air. The words I do not clearly recall; there was something about

> The sweet fields of Eden,
> On the other side of Jordan,

and a chorus ending in "hallelujah." I seemed to float upward on the wings of that melody, beyond the starry depths, through the gates of pearl, until it seemed to mingle with the sublime doxologies of the great multitude of the glorified that no one can number.

"What opera can equal that? There is a religious melody that has a quality of its own which no art can imitate."

The Bishop's thought was not new, but I had a new perception of its truth at that moment.

One of the converts of this camp-meeting was Levi Vanslyke. A wilder mustang was never caught by the gospel lasso. (Excuse this figure—it suits the case.) He was what was termed a "capper" to a gambling-hell in the town. Tall, excessively angular, jerky in movement, with singularly uneven features, his face and figure were very striking. He drifted with the crowd to the camp-ground one night, and his destiny was changed. He never went back to gambling. His conscience was awakened, and his soul mightily stirred, by the preaching, prayers, and songs. Amid the wonder and smiles of the crowd, he rose from his seat, went forward, and kneeled among the penitents, exhibiting signs of deep distress. An arrow of conviction had penetrated his heart, and brought him down at the foot of the cross. There he knelt, praying. The services were protracted far into the night, exhortations, songs, and prayers filling up the time. Suddenly Vanslyke rose from his knees with a bound, his face beaming with joy, and indulged in demonstrations which necessitated the suspension of all other exercises. He shouted and praised God, he shook hands with the brethren.

he exhorted his late associates to turn from their wicked ways—in fact, he took possession of the camp-ground, and the regular programme for the occasion was entirely superseded. The wild Vallecito "boys" were awe-struck, and quailed under his appeals.

Vanslyke was converted, a brand plucked from the burning. No room was left for doubt. He abandoned his old life at once. Soon he felt inward movings to preach the gospel, and began to study theology. He was a hard student, if not an apt one, and succeeded in passing the examinations (which in those days were not very rigid), and in due time was standing as a watchman on the walls of Zion. He was a faithful and useful minister of Jesus Christ. There was no backward movement in his religious life. He was faithful unto death, taking the hardest circuits uncomplainingly, always humble, self-denying, and cheerful, doing a work for his Master which many a showier man might covet in the day when He will reckon with His servants. He traveled and preached many years, a true soldier of Jesus Christ. He died in great peace, and is buried among the hills of Southern Oregon.

An episode connected with this camp-meeting was a visit to the Big Tree Grove of Calaveras. Every reader is familiar with descriptions of this wonderful forest, but no description can give an adequate impression of its solemn grandeur and beauty. The ride from Murphy's Camp in the early morning; the windings of the road among the colossal and shapely pines; the burst of wonder and delight of some of our party, and the silent yet perhaps deeper enjoyment of others, as we rode into the midst of the Titanic grove—all this made an experience which cannot be transferred to the printed page. The remark of the thoughtful woman who walked by my side expressed the sentiment that was uppermost in my own consciousness as I contemplated these wonders of the Almighty's handiwork: "God has created one spot where he will be worshiped, and it is this!"

THE TRAGEDY AT ALGERINE.

HOW Algerine Camp got its name I cannot tell. It was named before my day in California. The miners called it simply "Algerine," for short. They had a peculiar way of abbreviating all proper names. San Francisco was "Frisco," Chinese Camp was "Chinee," and Jamestown was "Jimtown." So Algerine was as many syllables as could be spared for this camp, whose fame still lingers as one of the richest, rowdiest, bloodiest camps of the Southern mines. Situated some seven or eight miles from Sonora, if in the early days it did not rival that lively city in size, it surpassed it in the recklessness with which its denizens gave themselves up to drinking, fighting, gambling, and general licentiousness. The name suited the place, whatever may have been its etymology. It was at the height of its glory for rich diggings and bad behavior in 1851. Lucky strikes and wild doings were the order of the day. A tragedy at "Algerine" ceased to excite more than a feeble interest—tragedies there had become commonplace. The pistol was the favorite weapon with the Algerines, but the monotony of shooting was now and then broken by a stabbing affair, of which a Mexican or native Californian was usually the hero. It was a disputed point whether the revolver or the dirk was the safer and more effective weapon in a free fight. Strong arguments were used on both sides of this interesting question, and popular opinion in the camp vacillated, taking direction according to the result of the last encounter.

With all its wickedness, Algerine had a public opinion and moral code of its own. The one sin that had no forgiveness was stealing. The remaining nine of the Ten Commandments nobody seemed to remember, but a stand was taken upon the eighth. Men that swore, ignored the Sabbath, gambled, got drunk, and were ready to use the pistol or knife on the slightest pretext, would flame with virtuous rage, and clamor for capital punishment, if a sluice were robbed, or the least article of any sort stolen. A thief was more completely outlawed than a murderer. The peculiar conditions existing, and the genius of the country, combined to develop this anomalous public sentiment, which will be illustrated by an incident that occurred in the year above referred to.

About 9 o'clock one morning, a messenger was seen riding at full speed through the main street of Sonora, his horse panting, and white with foam. He made his way to the sheriff's office, and on the appearance of one of the deputies, cried—well, I won't give his exact words, for they are not quotable; but the substance of his message was that a robbery had been committed at Algerine, that a mob had collected, and that one of the supposed robbers was in their hands.

"Hurry up, Captain, or you'll be too late to do any good—the camp is just boiling!"

Captain Stuart, the deputy-sheriff, was soon in the saddle, and on the way to Algerine. Stuart was a soldierly-looking man, over six feet high, square-shouldered, brawny, and with a dash of gracefulness in his bearing. He had fought in the war with Mexico, was known to be as brave as a lion, and was a general favorite. On a wider field he has since achieved a wider fame.

"There they are, Captain," said the messenger, pointing to the hill overlooking the camp from the north.

"My God! it's only a boy!" exclaimed Stuart, as his eye took in the scene.

Stripped of all but his shirt and white pants, bareheaded and barefooted, with a rope around his neck, the other end of which was held by a big, brutal-looking fellow in a blue flannel shirt, stood the victim of mob fury. He could scarcely be more than eighteen years old. His boyish face was pale as death, and was turned with a pleading look toward the huge fellow who held the rope, and who seemed to be the leader of the mob. He had begged hard for his life, and many hearts had been touched with pity.

"It's a shame, boys, to hang a child like that," said one, with a choking voice.

"It would be an eternal disgrace to the camp to allow it," said another.

Immediately surrounding the prisoner there was a growing party anxious to save him, whose intercessions had made quite a delay already. But the mob were blood-thirsty, and loud in their clamor for the hanging to go on.

"Up with him!" "What are you waiting for?" "Lift him, Bill!" and similar demands were made by a hundred voices at once.

In the midst of this contention Stuart, having dismounted, pushed his way by main strength through the crowd, and reached the side of the prisoner, whose face brightened with hope as the tall form of the officer of the law towered above him.

The appearance of the officer seemed to excite the mob, and a rush was made for the prisoner amid a storm of oaths and yells. Stuart's eye kindled as he cried—

"Keep back, you hounds! I'll blow out the brains of the first man that touches this boy!"

The front rank of the mob paused, keeping in check the yelling crowd behind them. The big fellow holding the rope kept his eye on Stuart, and seemed for the moment ready to surrender the honors of leadership to anybody who was covetous of the same. The cowardly brute quailed before a brave man's glance. He still held the rope, but kept his face averted from his intended victim.

Stuart, taking advantage of the momentary silence, made an earnest appeal to the mob. Pointing to the pale and trembling boy, he reminded them that he was only a youth, the mere tool and victim of the older criminals who had made their escape. To hang him would be simply murder, and every one who might have a hand in it would be haunted by the crime through life.

"Men, you are mad when you talk of hanging a mere boy like that. Are you savages? Where is your manhood? Instead of murdering him, it would be better to send him back to his poor old mother and sisters in the States."

The central group, at this point, presented a striking picture. The poor boy standing bareheaded in the sun, looking, in his white garments, as if he were already shrouded, gazing wistfully around; Stuart holding the crowd at bay, standing like a rock, his tall form erect, his face flushed, and his eye flashing; the burly leader of the mob, rope in hand, his coarse features expressing mingled fear and ferocity; the faces of the rabble, some touched with compassion, others turned upon the prisoner threateningly, while the great mass of them wore only that look of thoughtless animal excitement which makes a mob at once so dangerous and so contemptible a thing—all made a scene for an artist.

Again cries of "Up with him!" "Hang him!" "No more palaver!" were raised on the outer ranks of the mob, and another rush was made toward the prisoner. Stuart's voice and eye again arrested the movement. He appealed to their manhood and mercy in the most persuasive and impassioned manner, and it was evident that his appeals were not without effect on some of the men nearest to him. Seeing this, several of the more determined ruffians, with oaths and cries of fury, suddenly rushed forward with such impetuosity that Stuart was borne backward by their weight, the rope was grasped by several hands at once, and the prisoner was jerked with such violence as to pull him off his feet.

At this moment the sound of horses' hoofs was heard, and in another instant the reckless daredevil, Billy Worth, mounted on a powerful bay, pistol in hand, had opened a lane through the crowd, and quick as thought he cut the rope that bound the prisoner, and, with the assistance of two or three friendly hands, lifted him into the saddle before him, and galloped off in the direction of Sonora. The mob was paralyzed by the audacity of this proceeding, and attempted no immediate pursuit. The fact is, Worth's reputation as a desperate fighter and sure shot was such that none of them had any special desire to get within range of his revolver. If his virtues had equaled his courage, Billy Worth's name would have been one of the brightest on the roll of California's heroes. At this time he was an *attaché* of the sheriff's office, and was always ready for such desperate service. He never paused until he had his prisoner safely locked in jail at Sonora.

The mob dispersed slowly and sullenly, and, as the sequel proved, still bent on mischief.

The next morning the early risers in Sonora were thrilled with horror to find the poor boy hanging by the neck from a branch of an oak on the hill-side above the City Hotel. The Algerine mob had reörganized, marched into town at dead of night, overpowered the jailer, taken out their victim, and hung him. By sunrise, thousands, drawn by the fascination of horror, had gathered to the spot. And now that the poor lad was hanging there dead, there was only pity felt for his horrid fate, and detestation of the crime committed by his cruel murderers. The body was cut down and tenderly buried, women's hands placing flowers upon his coffin, and women's tears falling upon the cold face.

A singular fact must be added to this narrative. The tree on which the boy was hanged was a healthy, vigorous young oak, in full leaf. *In a few days its every leaf had withered!* This statement is made on the testimony of respectable living witnesses, whose reputation for veracity is unquestioned. The next year the tree put forth its buds and leaves as usual. This fact is left to the incredulity, superstition, or scientific inquiry of the reader. The tree may be still standing, as a memento of a horrible crime.

CALIFORNIA TRAITS.

CALIFORNIANS of the golden decades have never been surpassed in spontaneous, princely generosity. If a miner got hurt by a "cave," or premature explosion, it only took a few hours to raise five hundred or a thousand dollars for his widow. The veriest sot or tramp had only to get sick to be supplied with all that money could buy. There never was another people so open-handed to poverty, sickness, or the stranger. They were wild, wicked fellows, and made sad havoc of the larger part of the decalogue; but if deeds of charity are put to the credit of sinners, the Recording Angel smiled with inward joy as he put down many an item on the credit side of the eternal ledger. This trait distinguished all alike—saints and sinners, merchants and miners, gamblers and politicians, Jews and Gentiles, Yankees and Southerners, natives and foreigners. Here and there would be found a mean, close-fisted fellow, who never responded to the appeals of that heavenly charity which kept the hearts of those feverish, excited, struggling men alive. But such a man was made to feel that he was an object of intense scorn. The hot-tempered adventurer who shot down his enemy in fair fight could be tolerated, but not the miserly wretch who hoarded the dollar needed to save a fellow-man from want. Those Californians of the earlier days showed two traits in excess—a princely courage and a princely generosity; and their descendants will have in their traditions of them a source of inspiration that will serve to perpetuate among them a brave and generous manhood.

A notable exhibition of this spontaneous and princely generosity in the Californians took place in 1867. The war had left the South decimated, broken, impoverished—a land of grief and of graves. Already in 1866 the gaunt specter of Famine hovered over the fated South. The next year a general drought completed the catastrophe. The crops failed, there was no money, the war had stripped the Southern people of all but their lives and their land. It was a dark day. Starvation menaced hundreds of thousands of men, women, and children. By telegraph, by newspaper correspondents, and by private letters, the distressing news reached California.

A poor widow in Sonoma county, reading in the newspapers the accounts given of the suffering in the South, sent me six dollars and fifty cents, with a note saying she had earned the money by taking in washing. She added that it was but a mite, but it would help a little, leaving it to my discretion to send it where it was most needed. Her modest note was published in *The Christian Spectator*, of which I was then editor. The publication of that little note was like touching a spark to dry prairie grass. The hearts of the Californians were ready for the good work, and the poor Sonoma widow showed them the way to do it. From all parts of the State money poured in—by hundreds, by thousands, by tens of thousands of dollars, until directly and indirectly over ninety thousand dollars in gold was sent to the various relief committees in Baltimore, Macon, Nashville, Richmond, and other cities. The transmission of all this money cost not a dollar. The express companies carried the coin free of charge, the bankers remitted all charges on exchange—all services were rendered gratuitously.

The whole movement was carried out in true Californian style. A single incident will illustrate the spirit in which it was done. A week or two after the widow's note had been published, I had occasion to visit San Jose. It was Saturday, the great day for traffic in that flourishing city. The streets were thronged with vehicles and horses, and men and women, sauntering, trading, talking, gazing. The great center of resort was the junction of Santa Clara and First streets. As I was pushing my way through the dense mass of human beings at this point, I met Frank Stewart*—filibuster, philosopher, mineralogist, and editor.

"Wait here a moment," said Stewart to me.

Springing into an empty express-wagon, he cried "O yes," "O yes," "O yes," after the manner of sheriffs. The crowd gathered around him with inquiring looks. I stood looking on, wondering what he meant.

"Fellow-citizens," said Stewart, "while you are here enjoying prosperity and plenty, there is want in the homes of the South. Men, women, and children there are starving. They are our own countrymen—bone of our bone, and flesh of our flesh. We must send them help, and we must send it promptly. I tell you they are starving! In many homes this very night hungry children will sob themselves to sleep without food! But yonder I see an old neighbor, whom you all know," pointing to me; "he has recently visited the South, is in direct communication with it, and will be able to

---

*Stewart was with Walker in Nicaragua, and wrote an entertaining narrative of that romantic and tragic historical episode, entitled "The Last of the Filibusters."

give us the facts in the case. Get up here where you can be seen and heard, and tell us what you know of the distress in the South."

I attempted a retreat, but in vain. Almost before I knew it they had me on the express-wagon, talking to the crowd. It was a novel situation to me, and I felt awkward at first. The whole proceeding was a surprise. But there was sympathy and encouragement in the upturned faces of those Californians, and I soon felt at ease standing in my strange pulpit in the open air. My audience kept growing, the people deserting the street auctioneers, the stores, the saloons, and the sidewalks, and pressing close around the express-wagon. After describing scenes I had witnessed, I was giving some details of the latest news from the distressed localities, when a dark-skinned, grave-looking little man pressed his way through the crowd, and silently laid a five-dollar gold-piece on the seat of the express-wagon, at my feet. The effect was electric. Another, another, and another followed. Not a word was spoken, but strong breasts heaved with emotion, and many a bronzed cheek was wet. I could not go on with my speech, but broke down completely. Still the money poured in. It seemed as if every man in that vast throng had caught the feeling of the moment, as the Angel of Mercy hovered over the spot, and shed the dews of heaven from her shining wings. Never, even in the consecrated temple, amid worshiping hundreds, and pealing anthems, and fervent prayers, have I felt that God was nearer than at that moment. At length there was a pause. Mr. Spring, the lively and good-natured auctioneer, rushed into his store across the street, and bringing out a gaily-painted little cask of California wine, put it into my hands, saying—

"Sell this for the benefit of the cause."

This was indeed a new *role* to me. Taking the cask in my hands, and lifting it up before the crowd, I asked—

"Who will give five dollars for this cask of wine, the money to go to help the starving?"

"I will," said a man from Ohio, standing directly in front of me, advancing and laying down the money as he spoke.

"Who else will give five dollars for it?"

"I will"—"And I"—"And I"—"And I"—the responses came thick and fast, until the gallon-cask of wine had brought in eighty-five dollars. The last purchaser, a tall, good-natured fellow from Maine, said to me as he turned and walked off—

"Take the cask home with you, and keep it as a memento of this day."

The crowd scattered, and I gathered and counted the silver and gold that lay at my feet. It filled the canvas sack furnished by a friendly storekeeper, and ran high up into the hundreds. That was California—the California in which still lingered the spirit of the early days. I descended from my impromptu rostrum, invoking a benediction upon them and their children, and their children's children, and it is reëchoed in my heart as I write these lines, thousands of miles away on the banks of the Cumberland in Tennessee.

It ought to be added here that, in this work of relief for the South, Northern men and women were not a whit behind those from the South. The first subscriber to the fund, and the most active worker in its behalf in San Francisco, was Thomas H. Selby, a New-Yorker of noble and princely spirit, whose subsequent death robbed California of one of its richest jewels. I am glad to claim national kinship with such men and women.

On the afternoon before Thanksgiving-day, in eighteen hundred and sixty-something, two little girls came into my office, on Washington street. One was a chubby, curly-headed little beauty, about five years old. The other was a crippled child, about ten, with a pale, suffering face, and earnest, pleading blue eyes. She walked with crutches, and was out of breath when she got to the top of the long, narrow staircase in the third story of Reese's building, where I dispensed "copy" for the printer and school law for the pedagogues in those days.

The older girl handed me a note which she had brought in her thin, white hand. I opened the paper, and read these words—

"I am lying sick on Larkin street, near Sacramento, and there is not a mouthful to eat or cent of money in the house."

I recognized the signature as that of a man I had met at the Napa Springs two years before; he was then, as now, an invalid.

I took my hat and cane, and followed the children. It was painful work for the crippled girl, climbing the hill in the face of the heavy wind from the sea. Often she had to pause and rest a few moments, panting for breath, and trembling from weakness. When we reached the house, which was a rickety shanty, partly buried in the sand, a hollow-eyed, hopeless-looking woman met us at the door. She had the dull, weary look of a woman worn out with care and loss of rest. On a coarse bedstead lay the invalid. As soon as he saw me he pulled the quilt over his head, and gave way to his feelings. His sobs fairly shook the frail tenement. Looking around, I was shocked to see the utter absence of every thing necessary to the comfort of a family. They had parted with every article that would bring a little money with which to buy food. Where the children, five in number, slept I could not conceive. Making a short stay,

I went forth to send them relief. A genial, redbearded New Hampshire man kept a grocery and provision store on the corner of Jackson and Stockton streets. I liked him, and sometimes patronized him. I gave him the address of the needy family, and instructed him to send them every thing they needed. Before sunset a heavy-laden wagon deposited such stores of eatables at the sandhill shanty as made the inmates thereof wonder. When the bill was presented, it was evident that he had not charged half-price. I knew my man.

The next day my purpose was to go to Calvary Church and hear a sermon from the brilliant Dr. Charles Wadsworth, with whom striking and eloquent thanksgiving-sermons had long been a specialty. On my way to church I thought of the helpless family in the sand-hills, and I resolved to change my thanksgiving programme. The thought was suggested to my mind that I would go up one side of Montgomery street and down the other, and ask every acquaintance I should happen to meet for a contribution to my *protégés* on Larkin street. The day was lovely, and all San Francisco was on the streets. (You must go to California to learn how delightful a November day can be.) Before I had gone two squares so much specie had been given me that I found it necessary to get a sack to hold it. On the corner of California street I came upon Colonel Eyre and a knot of other brokers, ten in number, every one of whom gave me a five-dollar gold-piece. By the time I had gotten back to my starting-point on the corner of Washington street, the canvas sack was full of gold and silver. I took it at once to Larkin street.

The sad, hollow-eyed woman met me at the door. I handed her the sack—she felt its weight, began to tremble, staggered to the bed, and sinking down upon it, burst into a fit of violent weeping. The reaction was too sudden for her—poor, worn creature! The sick man also cried, and the children cried—and I am not sure my own eyes were dry. I left them very soon, and wended my way homeward to my cottage on the western edge of Russian Hill, above the sea. My thanksgiving-dinner was enjoyed that day.

About seven years afterward a man overtook me on the street in San Francisco, and grasping my hand warmly, called me by name:

"Don't you know me? Don't you remember the man to whom you brought that money on thanksgiving-day, seven years ago? I'm the man. That money made my fortune. I was able to obtain medicines and comforts which before I had not the means to buy; my mind was relieved of its load of terrible mental anxiety; my health began to improve from that day, and now I am a well man, prosperous in business, and with as happy a family around me as there is on earth."

What more he said, as he held and pressed my hand, need not be repeated.

If we search for the cause of this Californian trait of character, perhaps it may be found in the fact that the early Californians were mostly adventurers. (Please remember that this word has a good as well as a bad sense.) Their own vicissitudes and wrestlings with fortune gave them a vivid realization of the feelings of a fellow-man struggling with adversity. It was a great Brotherhood of Adventure, from whose fellowship no man was excluded. They would fight to the death over a disputed claim; they would too often make the strong hand the test of right; they gave their animal passions free play, and enacted bloody tragedies. But they never shut their purses against the distressed, nor turned a deaf ear to the voice of sorrow. Doubtless the case and rapidity with which fortunes were made in the early days also contributed to produce this free-handedness. A man who made, or hoped to make, a fortune in a week, did not stop to count the money he spent on his schemes, his passions, or his charities. Cases came to my knowledge in which princely fortunes were squandered by a week of debauch with cards, wine, and women.

A sailor struck a "pocket" on Wood's Creek, and took out forty thousand dollars in two days. He went into town, deposited the dust, drew several thousand dollars in coin, and entered upon a debauch. In a day or two the coin was exhausted, the gamblers, saloon-keepers, and bad women having divided it between them. Half-crazed with drink, he called for his gold-dust, and taking it to the "Long Tom," he began to bet heavily against a faro-bank. Staking handfuls of the shining dust, he alternately won and lost, until, becoming excited beyond control, he staked the entire sack of gold-dust, valued at twenty-eight thousand dollars, on a single card, and—lost, of course. He went to bed and slept off the fumes of his drunkenness, got money enough to take him to San Francisco, where he shipped as a common sailor on a vessel bound for Shanghai. He expressed no regret for the loss of his treasure, but boasted that he had a jolly time while it lasted.

In Sonora there was a rough, whisky-loving fellow, named Bill F——, who divided his time between gambling, drinking, and deer-hunting. One day he took his rifle and sallied forth in search of venison. He wandered among the hills for several hours without finding any game. Reaching a projection of Bald Mountain, a few hundred yards below the summit, tired and hot, he threw himself on the ground to rest under the shade of a stunted tree. In an idle way he began to dig into the rotten quartz with his hunting-knife, thinking such thoughts as would come into the mind of such a harum-scarum fellow under the circumstances.

"What's this?" he suddenly exclaimed. "Hurrah! I have struck it! It's gold! It's gold!"

And so it was gold. Bill had struck a "pocket," and a rich one. His deer-hunt was a lucky one after all. Marking well the spot, he lost no time in hurrying back to Sonora, where he provided himself with a strong, iron-bound water-bucket, and then returned with his treasure, which amounted to forty thousand dollars. The "pocket" was exhausted. Though much labor and money were expended in the search, no more gold could be found there. Bill took his gold to town, and was the hero of the hour. But one way of celebrating his good fortune occurred to his mind. He went on a big spree—whisky, cards, etc. He was a quarrelsome and ugly fellow when drinking. The very next day he got into a fight at the City Hotel, and was shot dead, leaving the most of his bucketful of gold-dust unspent. The time and manner of Bill's death was, in its result, the best thing known of his history. A strange thing happened: the money found its way to his mother in Pennsylvania, every dollar of it. Public sentiment aided the public administrator in doing his duty in this case. It was a common saying among the Californians in those days, that when an estate was taken charge of by that functionary, the legal heirs had small show of getting any part of it. The temptation was great in many cases. Men died suddenly, leaving neither partner nor kinsman to look after the large possessions they left behind, and these vultures were not slow in finding their prey. Public sentiment was lax at this point, and perhaps naturally. Living men were too busy and too much excited with their schemes to think much of the estates of dead ones, and so if a dishonest man got into the office of public administrator, "the devil of opportunity" was sure to meet and overcome him. It is but just to say, however, that there was a latent moral sense among the Californians that never failed to condemn the faithless public servant. They did not take time to prosecute him, but they made him feel that he was despised.

CALIFORNIA WEDDINGS.

IF the histories connected with the California weddings that I have attended could be written out in full, what tragedies, comedies, and farces would excite the tears and laughter of the susceptible reader! Orange blossoms and pistols are mingled in the matrimonial retrospect. The sound of merry wedding-bells, the wails of heart-broken grief, and the imprecations of desperate hate, echo in the ear of memory as I begin this chapter on California Weddings. Nothing else could give a better picture of the vanishing phases of the social life of California. But prudence and good taste restrain my pencil. Too many of the parties are still living, and the subject is too delicate, to allow entire freedom of delineation. A guarded glance is all that may be allowed. No real names will be called.

Mounted on "Old Frank" one clear, bracing morning in 1856, I was galloping along the highway between Peppermint Gulch and Sonora, when I overtook a lawyer named G——, who was noted for his irascible temper and too ready disposition to fight, but whose talents and energy had won for him a leading position at the bar. It was an exhilarating ride as we dashed on at a swinging pace, the cool breeze kissing our faces, the blue sky above, the surrounding hills softened by shadows at their bases and glowing with sunshine on their tops. The reader who has never had a gallop among the foot-hills of California in clear weather has missed one of life's supremest pleasures. The air is electric, every nerve tingles, the blood seems turned to ether. You feel as you do when you fly in dreaming. It is not merely pleasure, it is ecstasy!

But little was said by us. The pace was too rapid for conversation, and neither of us was in the mood for commonplaces. My fellow-horseman's face, usually wearing half a sneer and half a frown, bore an expression I had never seen on it before. It was an expression of gentleness and thoughtfulness, and it became him so well that I found myself frequently turning to look at him. Suddenly reining in his horse, he cried to me—

"Stop, parson; I have something to say to you."

Checking "Old Frank," I waited for him to come up with me.

"Will you be at home to-morrow?"

"Yes, I shall be at home."

"Then come to this address at 1 o'clock, prepared to perform a marriage ceremony."

Penciling the address on a slip of paper, he handed it to me, and we rode on, resuming the rapid gallop which was the only gait known to the early Californians.

The next day I was punctual to the appointment. In the parlor of one of the coziest little cottages in the lower part of the city I found a number of lawyers, and other well-known citizens, with several women. The room was tastefully decorated with flowers of exquisite odor. A beautiful little girl about four years old came into the apartment. Richly and tastefully dressed, perfectly formed, elastic and graceful in her movements, with dark eyes, brilliant and large, and cheeks glowing with health, she was a sweet picture of fresh and innocent childhood. She looked around upon the guests, shyly declining the caresses that were offered her. Taking a seat by one of the women, she sat silent and wondering.

"Is n't she a perfect beauty!" said Dr. A——, whose own subsequent marriage made a strange chapter in the social annals of the place.

"Yes, she is a little queen, and I am glad for her sake that this little affair is to come off," said another.

In a few minutes G—— entered the room with a woman on his arm. She was fair and slender, with a weak mouth and nervous manner. Traces of tears were on her cheeks, but she was smiling. The company rose as I advanced to meet them, and remained standing while the solemn ceremony was being pronounced which made them husband and wife. When the last words were said, they kissed each other, and then G——, yielding to a sudden impulse, caught up the little girl in his arms, and almost smothered her with passionate kisses. Not a word was spoken, but many eyes were wet.

The guests were soon led into another room, in which a sumptuous repast was spread, and when I left champagne corks were popping, and it was evident that the lately silent company had found their tongues. Toasts, songs, and speeches were said and sung in honor of the joyful event just consummated—the marriage of this couple which ought to have taken place five years sooner. A little child had led the sinners back into the path from which through passion and weakness they had strayed.

It was after 9 o'clock one night in the fall of the same year that, hearing a knock at the door, I opened it, and found that my visitor was Edward C——, a young man who was working a mining claim on Dragoon Gulch, near town.

"Annie B—— and I intend to get married tonight, and we want you to perform the ceremony," he said, not waiting for ordinary salutations.

"Is n't this a strange and sudden affair?"

"Yes, it is a runaway match. Annie is under age, and her guardian will not give his consent."

"If that is the case, you will have to go to somebody else. The law is plain, and I cannot violate it."

"When you know all the facts, you will think differently."

He then proceeded to give me the facts in the case, which, briefly told, were these: He and Annie B—— loved each other, and had been engaged for several months, with the understanding that they were to be married when she should come of age. Annie had a few thousand dollars in the hands of her brother-in-law, who was also her legal guardian. This brother-in-law had a brother, a drunken, gambling, worthless fellow, whom he wished Annie to marry. She loathed him, and repelled the proposition with indignation and scorn. The brother and brother-in-law persisted in urging the hateful suit, having, it was thought, fixed a covetous eye on Annie's convenient little patrimony. Force had even been used, and Annie was deprived of her liberty and locked in her room. Her repugnance to the fellow increased the more he tried to make himself agreeable to her. A stormy scene had taken place that day.

"I will never marry him—never! I will die first!" Annie had exclaimed in a burst of passion, at the close of a long altercation.

"You are a foolish, undutiful girl, and will be made to do it!" was the angry reply of the brother-in-law as he turned the key in the door and closed the interview.

Late that afternoon Annie was on the street with her sister, and meeting her lover, they arranged to be married at once. She went to the house of a friendly family, while he undertook to get a minister and make other preparations for the event.

"This is the situation," said the expectant bridegroom. "The only way by which I can get the right to protect Annie is to marry her. If you will not perform the ceremony, we'll get a justice of the peace to do it. Annie shall never go back to that house. We intend to be married this night, come what may!"

I confess I liked his spirit, and my sympathies responded to the appeal made to them. He seemed to read as much in my face, for he added in an off-hand way—

"Get your hat and come along. They are all waiting for you at D——'s."

On reaching the house I found that quite a little company of intimate friends had been summoned, and the diminutive sitting-room was crowded with men, women, and children. The bride was seated in the midst, a pretty, blue-eyed, fair-complexioned girl of seventeen. As I looked at her, I could not blame her lover for risking something for such a prize. Women were then at a premium in the mines, and such lovely specimens as Annie would have been in demand anywhere. She blushed and smiled at the rather rough jokes of which she was made the subject by the good-natured company present, and when she stood up with C—— to take the vows that were to unite them for life, they were a handsome and happy pair.

The ceremony finished, the congratulations were hearty, the blushing bride having to stand a regular osculatory fire, according to the custom. Refreshments were then distributed, and seated on the bed, on chairs, stools, and boxes, drafted for the occasion, the delighted guests gave themselves up to social enjoyment.

"What is that?" exclaimed a dozen voices at once, as the most terrific sounds burst forth all around the house, as if Pandemonium had broken loose. The bride, whose nerves had already been under high tension all day, fainted, the women screamed, and the children yelled with fright.

"It's only a *charivari*" (*shivaree*, Anglice), said

the tall, red-headed head of the family, grinning. "I was afraid the boys would find out what was going on."

In the meantime the discord raged outside. It seemed as if every thing that could make a particularly unpleasant sound had been brought into service — tin pans, cracked horns, crippled drums, squeaking whistles, fiddles out of tune, accordions not in accord, bagpipes that seemed to know that they must do their worst—the whole culminating in the notes of a single human voice, the most vile and discordant ever heard. It was equally impossible not to be angry, and not to laugh. The bridegroom, an excitable man of Celtic blood, taking the demonstration as an insult, threatened to shoot into the crowd of musicians, but was persuaded to adopt a milder course, namely, to treat. That was the law in the mines, and it was a bold man who would try to evade it. The only means of escape was utter secrecy, and somehow or other it is next to impossible to conceal an impending wedding. It is a sweet secret that the birds of the air will whisper, and it becomes the confidential possession of the entire community. Opening the door, C—— was greeted by a cheer, the music ceasing for the moment.

"Come, boys, let's go to the Placer Hotel and take something," said he, forcing a cheerful tone.

Three cheers for the bridegroom and bride were proposed and given with a will, and the party filed away in the darkness, their various instruments of discord emitting desultory farewell notes, the last heard being the tootings of a horn that seemed to possess a sort of ventriloquial quality, sounding as if it were blown under ground.

The brother-in-law made no opposition to the wedding. Public opinion was too clearly against him. All went smoothly with the young married couple. It was a love-match, and they were content in their little one-roomed cottage at the foot of the hill. When I last heard from them they were living near the same spot, poor but happy, with a family of eleven children, ranging from a fair-haired girl of nineteen, the counterpart of Annie B—— in 1856, to a chubby little Californian of three summers, who bears the image and takes the name of his father.

While busily engaged one day in mailing the weekly issue of the *Pacific Methodist*, at the office near the corner of Montgomery and Jackson streets, San Francisco, a dusty, unshaved man with a slouched hat came into the room. His manner was sheepish and awkward, and my first impression was that he wanted to borrow money. There is a peculiar manner about habitual borrowers which is readily recognized after some experience with them. My visitor sat and toyed with his hat, making an occasional remark about the weather and other commonplaces. I answered affably, and kept on writing. At length, with a great effort, he said—

"Do you know anybody about here that can marry folks?"

I answered in the affirmative.

"May be you *mought* do it?" he said inquiringly.

I told him I thought I "mought," being a minister of the gospel.

"Well, come right along with me. The woman is waiting at the hotel, and there's no time to lose —the boat leaves at 2 o'clock."

Seeing me making some adjustment of a disordered neck-tie, he said impatiently—

"Don't wait to fix up—I tell you the boat leaves at 2 o'clock!"

I followed him to the Tremont House, and as we entered the parlor he said—

"Git up, old lady; that thing can be put through now"—addressing a very stout, middle-aged woman with a frowzy head, sitting near a window.

The lady addressed in this off-hand way rose to her feet and took her place by the side of the not very bridegroomish gentleman who had been my conductor.

"Do you not want any witnesses?" I asked.

"We haven't time to wait for witnesses—the boat will leave at 2 o'clock," said the man. "Go on with your ceremony."

I began the ceremony, she looking triumphant and defiant, and he subdued and despondent. There were two children in the room—a freckled-faced boy and a girl, the boy *minus* an eye, and their peculiar behavior attracted my attention. They kept circling around the bridal party, eyeing me curiously and resentfully, the one eye of the boy giving him a look both comic and sinister. The woman's responses were loud and strong, the man's feeble and low. Evidently he did not enjoy the occasion—he was marrying under inward protest. (The landlord's explanation accounted for that, but it is withheld here.)

"What do you charge for that?" said the bridegroom, as I concluded the ceremony.

I made some conventional remark about "the pleasure of the occasion being an ample compensation," or words to that effect. In the meantime he had with some difficulty untied a well-worn buckskin purse, from which he took a ten-dollar goldpiece which he tendered me with the remark—

"Will that do?"

I took it. It would not have been respectful to decline.

"You may go now," said the newly-married man;

"the boat will start at 2 o'clock, and we must be off."

The whole transaction did not take more than ten minutes. I trust the bridal party did not miss that boat. The one-eyed boy gave me a malevolent look as I started down the stairs.

One day in 1869 a well-known public man came to my office and asked a private interview. Taking him into the rear room, and closing the door, I invited him to unfold his errand.

"There is trouble between my wife and me. The fact is, I have done wrong, and she has found it out. She is a good woman, but very peculiar, and if something is not done speedily I fear she will become deranged. I am uneasy about her now. She says nothing will satisfy her but for me to solemnly repeat, in the presence of a minister of the gospel, the marriage vows I have violated. I am willing to do any thing I can to satisfy her. Will you name an hour for us to call at your office for the purpose of being remarried?"

"The suggestion is such a strange one that I must have time to consider it. Come back at four this afternoon, and I will give you an answer."

I laid the case before a shrewd lawyer of my acquaintance, and asked his advice.

"Marry them, of course," said he at once. "The ceremony has no legal quality whatever, but it is the business of a clergyman to minister to a mind diseased, and it is your duty to comply with the unhappy woman's wish."

The gentleman returned at four, and I told him to come at ten the next morning, promising to perform the wished-for ceremony.

They came punctual to the minute. Excluding a number of visitors, I locked my office door on the inside, and gave my attention to the strange business before me. They both began to weep as I began solemnly to read the marriage service. What tender recollections of earlier and happier days crowded upon their minds, I know not. Their emotion increased, and they were sobbing in each other's arms when I had finished. She was radiant through her tears, while he looked like a repenting sinner who had received absolution. The form for the celebration of the office of holy matrimony, as laid down in the Ritual of my Church, never sounded so exquisitely beautiful, or seemed so impressive before; and when he put a twenty-dollar piece in my hand, and departed, I thought remarriage might be wise and proper under some circumstances.

I had the pleasure of officiating at the nuptials of a goodly number of my colored friends in San Francisco, from about 1857 to 1861. One of these occasions impressed me particularly. A venerable black man, who was a deacon in the colored Baptist Church on Dupont street, called at my office with a message requesting me to visit a certain number on Sacramento street, at a given hour, for the purpose of uniting his brother and a colored lady in marriage. Remembering the crude old English couplet which says that

> When a wedding's in the case,
> All else must give place,

I did not fail to be on time. The company were assembled in the large basement-room of a substantial brick house. A dozen or fifteen colored people were present, and several white ladies had gathered in the hall to witness the important ceremony. When the bridegroom and bride presented themselves, I was struck with their appearance. The bridegroom was a little old negro, not less than seventy years old, with very crooked legs, short forehead, and eyes scarcely larger than a pea, with a weird, "varmint-like" face, showing that it would not take many removes to trace his pedigree back to Guinea. The bride was a tall and well-formed young black woman, scarcely twenty years old, whose hair (or wool) was elaborately carded and arranged, and who wore a white dress, with a large red rose in her bosom. The aged bridegroom hardly reached her shoulders as she stood by him in gorgeous array. They made a ludicrous couple, and I observed a smile on the faces of the intelligent colored people standing around. He was the queerest bridegroom I had ever met, as he stood there peering about him with those curious little eyes. The bride herself seemed to take in the comic element of the occasion, for her fat face wore a broad grin. I began the ceremony, keeping down any tendency to unseemly laughter by throwing extra emphasis and solemnity into my voice. This is a device to which others have resorted under similar circumstances. Mastering my risibles, I was proceeding with elevated voice and special emphasis, when the bridegroom, looking up at me with those little beads of eyes, broke in with this remark, chuckling as he spoke—

"I ain't scared—*Ise been 'long here befo.*"

It was the first time I ever broke down in a serious service. We all laughed, the bridegroom and bride both joining in heartily, and the tittering did not subside until the ceremony was ended. Evidently the old sinner had a history. How often he had been married—after a fashion—it would have been hazardous to guess. No doubt he had been there before.

NORTH BEACH, SAN FRANCISCO.

NORTH BEACH, in its gentle mood, is as quiet as a Quaker maiden, and as lovely; but when fretted by the rude sea-wind, it is like a virago in her tantrums. I have looked upon it at the close of a bright, clear day, fascinated by the changing glories of a gorgeous sunset. The still ships seemed asleep upon the placid waters. Above the Golden Gate hung a drapery of burning clouds, almost too bright for the naked eye. Tamalpais,* towering above the Marin hills, wrapped in his evening robe of royal purple, sat like a king on his throne. The islands in sight, sunlit and calm, seemed to be dreaming in the soft embrace of the blue waters. Above the golden

---

* A lofty peak of the coast-range that shoots its bare summit high into the sky north of the bay, and within a few miles of the Golden Gate, from which the view is one of marvelous scope and surpassing beauty.

glow of the breezy Contra Costa hills the sky blushed rosy red, as if conscious of its own charms. As the sun sank into the Pacific in a blaze of splendor, the bugle of Fort Alcatraz, pealing over the waters, told that the day was done. And then the scene gradually changed. The cloud-fires that blazed above the Gate of Gold died out, the purple of Tamalpais deepened into blackness, in the thickening twilight the sunlit islands faded from sight, the rose-tinted sky turned into sober gray, the stars came out one by one, and a night of beauty followed a day of brightness. Many a time, from my bay-window, on such evenings as this, have I seen young men and maidens walking side by side, or hand in hand, along the beach, whispering words that only the sea might hear, and uttering vows that only the stars might witness. Here I have seen the weary man of business linger as if he were loth to leave a scene so quiet, and go back to the din, and rush, and worry of the city. And pale, sad-faced women in black have come alone to weep by the sea-side, and have gone back with the traces of fresh tears upon their cheeks, and the light of renewed hope in their eyes. On bright mornings, new-married couples, climbing the hill whose western declivity overlooks the Golden Gate and the vast Pacific, have felt that the immensity and calm of the ocean were emblematic of the serene and immeasurable happiness they had in each other. They might remember that even that Pacific sea is swept by storms, and that beneath its quiet waters lies many a noble ship, wrecked on its way to port. But they felt no fear, for there is no shipwreck of true love, human or divine; it always survives the storm.

North Beach, in its stormy mood, had also its fascination for the storm-tossed, and the desolate, and the despairing. It was hither that Ralston hurried on that fatal day when the crash came. His death was like his life. He was a strong swimmer, but he ventured too far. The wind sweeping in through the Golden Gate chill and angry, the white-capped waters of the bay in wild unrest, the gathering fog darkening the sky, were all symbolic of the days of struggle and the nights of anguish that preceded the final tragedy. He died struggling. If he had come out of that wrestle with the sea alive, he would have been on his feet to-day, for he embodied in himself the energy, the dash, the invincible courage of the true Californian. Ralston did not commit suicide. He was not a man of that type.

Sitting in my bay-window above the beach one stormy evening about sunset, my attention was arrested by the movements of a man sitting on the rocks in the edge of the water, where the spray drenched his person every time a wave broke against the shore. Suddenly he took a pistol from his pocket, placed the muzzle against his head, and fired. I sprang to my feet as he tumbled forward into the water, and rushed down the long steps, and reached the spot just as a refluent wave bore him back to the beach. Dragging him out of the water, it was found that he was still breathing, and had a faint pulse. The blood was oozing from an ugly bullet wound back of his right ear—the ball had struck the bone and slightly glanced. Brandy was brought, which he swallowed in large quantities; his pulse grew quicker and stronger, and looking around upon the curious and pitying group that had gathered about him, he seemed suddenly to comprehend the whole situation. With a desperate effort he rose to his feet, exclaiming—

"Why did n't you let me alone? If you had, it would all have been over now. Am I doomed to live against my will? The very sea refuses me a grave!"

I made some remark, with the view to calm and encourage him.

"You mean well, and I ought to thank you, sir; but you have done me an ill turn. I want to die, and get out of it all."

"What is the trouble, my friend?" I inquired, the question prompted by pity and curiosity.

He turned suddenly, stared at me a moment, and said fiercely—

"Never mind what my trouble is. It is what death only can relieve. Why did n't you let me die?"

He was a heavy-set man of fifty, with iron-gray whiskers, a good, open, intelligent face, and neatly dressed in a suit of gray cloth.

He reeled as he spoke, and would have fallen had he not been supported by kind hands. He was taken to the hospital, where the bullet was extracted from his head, and he got well. Who he was, and what was his story, was never found out. He kept his secret.

About sunrise one morning, looking out of my window, I saw a crowd huddled around some object on the beach. Their subdued behavior suggested a tragedy. The North Beach rabble, in its ordinary mood, is rather noisy and demonstrative. The hoodlum reaches his perfection here. The hoodlum is a young Californian in the intermediate stage between a wharf-rat and a desperado, combining all the bad qualities of both. He is dishonest, lewd, insolent, and unspeakably vulgar. He glories in his viciousness, and his swagger is inimitable. There is but one thing about him that has the semblance of a virtue, and that is his courageous fidelity to his fellow-hoodlums. He will defend one of his kind to the death in a street-fight, or swear to any thing to help him in a court of justice. This element is usually largely represented in any popular gathering at North Beach, but they were not numerous at that early hour. They run late at night, and are not early risers. But the women that sold beer on the flat, the men that drove dirt-carts, the fishermen who fished in the bay, and the crowd of fellows that lived nobody knew where, or how, that appear as by magic when an exciting event calls them forth, were all there as I made my way through the throng and reached the object that had drawn them to the spot.

It was a man hanging by his neck from the highest tier of a lot of damaged hay-bales that had been unloaded on the beach. He had come out there in the night, taken a piece of hay-rope, adjusted it to his neck with great skill, fastened it to a topmost bale of hay, and then leaped into eternity. It was a horrid spectacle. The man was a Frenchman, who had slept two nights in a recess of the hay-pile. The popular verdict was, insanity or starvation. From a look at the ghastly face, and poor, thin frame, with its tattered garments fluttering in the breeze, you might think it was both. The previous night had been colder than usual; perhaps hanging was to his mind a shorter and easier death than freezing. Nobody knows— he, too, kept his secret.

Almost opposite my bay-window was a large rock, which was nearly covered by the tide at high water, and over which the surf broke with great violence when a north wind drove the waters upon the beach. The North Beach breakers sometimes run so high as to send their spray over the high embankment of Bay street, and their thunder makes sublime music on a stormy night. One day when the bay was lashed into anger by a strong wind from the north-west, and the surf rolling in heavily, a slender young girl was seen hurrying along the beach with downcast look and a veil over her face. Without pausing, she waded through the surf and climbed the rock, and lifting her veil for a moment, and disclosing a pale, beautiful face as she cast a look at the sky, she threw herself into the sea, her veil floating away as she sank. A rush of the waves dashed her body back against the rock, and, as it swayed to and fro, fragments of her dress were visible. A passing cartman, who had witnessed her wild leap, plunged into the water, and with some difficulty caught the body, and brought it to the shore.

"Poor thing! She's only a child," said a red-faced, stout woman, who was the mistress of a notorious beer-house on the flat, but whose coarse features were softened into a pitying expression as she looked upon the fair, girlish face, and slender form lying at her feet, the blood running from two or three gashes cut by the sharp rocks upon her temple and forehead.

"God pity the darlin'! She's still alive," said another woman of the same class, as she stooped down and put her hand upon the girl's heart.

Lifting her tenderly in their strong arms, she was carried into a house close at hand, and by the use of proper means brought back to consciousness. What were her thoughts when she opened her eyes, and in the half-darkened room looked around upon the rough denizens of the flat, I know not. Her first thought may have been that she had awaked in the world so awfully pictured by the grand and gloomy Florentine. Hiding her face with her hands, she gave way to an agony of grief. Her secret was the old story. Though but a school-girl, she had loved, sinned, and despaired, her weakness and folly culminating in attempted self-murder. Beyond this no more will be told: I will keep her secret, having reason to hope that the young life which she tried to throw away at North Beach is not wholly blighted. She is scarcely out of her teens now.

Here a famous gambler, Tom H——, came in the early part of an afternoon, and lying down at the foot of the huge sand-hill above the beach, shot himself through the breast. A boatman found him lying on his back, the blood streaming from the wound and crimsoning the white sand. It was a woman that caused him thus to throw up the game of life. He was a handsome fellow, muscular, clean-limbed, and full-chested, but it was a sad spectacle as they drove him away in an open wagon, the blood dripping along the street, the poor fellow gasping and moaning so piteously. Recovering consciousness that night, he tore away the bandages with which his wound had been stanched, declaring he would die, for "the game was up." Before daybreak next morning he had his wish, and died.

Above us, on the hill-side, lived a family consisting of the mother, and father, and three children. One of the children was a bright, active little fellow, five or six years old, who had the quickest foot and merriest laugh of all the little people that were in the habit of gathering on the beach to pick up shells, or play in the moist sand, or toy with the waves as they ended in a fringe of foam at their feet. On a windy day the little fellow had gone down to the beach, and amused himself by watching the waves as they broke upon the embankment of the new street that was rising out of the sea. At one point there was a break in the embankment, leaving a passage for the waters that ebbed and flowed with the tide. A narrow plank was thrown across the place for foot-passengers. The little boy started to cross it just as a huge wave rolled in from the sea, and was struck by it, and carried by its force into the deep water beyond. His little playmates, paralyzed with terror, instead of giving the alarm at once, stood watching the spot where he went down. But at last the alarm was given, and a score of men plunged into the water and began to search for the child's body. A crowd gathered on the bank, looking on with the fascination that so singularly attracts men and women to the tragic and the horrible. At length a strong swimmer and good diver found the little body, and brought it to the shore. It was cold and stark, the eyes staring, the sunny curls matted over the marble brow, and his little jacket stained with the mud. One of the men took him in his arms, and, followed by the crowd, slowly ascended the hill. The mother was standing at the gate, wondering what such a procession meant, no one having had the presence of mind to prepare her for the blow. When she caught sight of the little face resting on the shoulder of the rough but kind-hearted man who carried the dead child, she shrieked, as she fell to the earth—

"O God! My child! my child!"

The spot where the child was drowned was in full view from the house, and the poor mother could see it every time she looked from her door or window. I was glad when the place was filled up, and a factory erected upon the fateful spot.

There is yet another aspect of North Beach that lingers in memory. I have lain awake during many a long night of bodily pain and mental anguish, listening to the plash of the waves as they broke gently upon the beach just below, and the music of the billows soothed my tortured nerves, and the voice of the mighty sea spoke to my troubled soul, as the voice of Him whose footsteps are upon the great waters, and whose paths are in the seas. And it was from our cottage at North Beach that we bore to the grave our child of suffering, our Paul, whose twenty summers were all clouded by affliction, but beautiful in goodness, and whose resting-place beside another little grave near San Jose makes us turn many a wistful look toward the sunset.

ST. HELEN'S AT SUNRISE.

(Written on the cars in Russian River Valley, California, at sunrise, February 4, 1873.)

THE shadows of darkness at day-break are flying,
   The clouds o'er the valley hang heavy and chill;
The morning-star fades, its pale gleam is dying,
   As the day-beams brighten o'er the wood-covered hill.

We swept down the valley as the night-curtain lifted,
   And the cold gray of morning spread over the sky,
And the clouds in thick masses the strong wind had drifted
   Up the sides of the mountains which towered so nigh.

Lo! a glory supernal! St. Helen's, snow-covered,
   White, silent, and awful, sat high on her throne;
The clouds at her foot, where the storm-angel hovered,
   The clear light revealing the sky-piercing cone.

O glory yet greater! The white, silent mountain,
   Transfigured with sunrise, flames out in the light
That beams on its face from its far-distant fountain,
   And bathes in full splendor its East-looking height.

My soul, in that moment so rapt and so holy,
   Was transfigured with Nature, and felt the deep spell;
My spirit, entranced, bent meekly and lowly
   With rapture that only an angel could tell.

When the night-mists of time around me are flying,
   When the shadows of death gather round me apace,
O Jesus, my Sun, shine on me when dying,
   Transfigure my soul with the light of thy face!

www.ingramcontent.com/pod-product-compliance
Lightning Source LLC
Chambersburg PA
CBHW051052160426
43193CB00010B/1153